D0459053

Country Chicken

The Results Are in— And the Winner Is *You!*

WITH forks and knives in hand, families across the country have been "voting" in a very special election lately.

Now, the mouth-watering results are in—in this brand-new cookbook you're holding. It contains over *250 recipes* for chicken *guaranteed* to get a finger-lickin'-good reaction.

You see, in putting together *Country Chicken*, we went to the experts on the subject—cooks just like you. We asked each to pick out the chicken dishes that routinely win requests for seconds (and thirds!) from her own hearty eaters...and then send us the *very* best of those—the *one* recipe her family would rate as her choicest chicken creation.

So there's no "filler" in this book. Every recipe's a certified "Can you make this again *soon?*" winner. And here's more good news—you can start cooking any of these recipes *right now*, because every one's made with ingredients you likely already have on hand.

What sorts of recipes will you find here? Well, folks in Wartrace, Tennessee rave about the crunchy coating on Mildred Troupe's Pecan Oven-Fried Fryer (recipe on page 36). Nancy Renaut's clan in Naperville, Illinois agrees that, after spending time outdoors, there's nothing better than sitting down to robust Creamy Chicken Stew (page 40).

The barbecue aroma of Jane MacKinnis' oven-baked Sweet Smoky Chicken Legs (page 55) always delights her family in Eden, Maryland. And DeAnna Steed's brood in Ignacio, Colorado can't resist Summer Squash Enchiladas (page 71)—a filling casserole featuring the season's finest produce.

Those are just a few of the *many* Country-Fried Favorites, Skillet Specialties, Oven Entrees and Comforting Casseroles inside. Plus, there are innovative ideas for hearty appetizers...refreshing salads...satisfying soups and sandwiches...and sizzling grilled goodies.

There's a Festive Family Fare chapter, too, that proves elegant entrees can also be easy to prepare. As an added feature, *Country Chicken* includes a number of recipes marked with a "✓" that use less salt, sugar and fat and include *Diabetic Exchanges*. So even folks on restricted diets can enjoy the country's top-tasting chicken.

In fact, with *Country Chicken*, you could prepare a new chicken dish almost every day of the week for a year and never repeat a recipe. But take the word of the hundreds of families who selected the contents of this book with their enthusiastic eating—once *your* family tastes these dishes, they won't let you wait anywhere near that long to make them again!

Editor: Julie Schnittka
Food Editor: Mary Beth Jung
Assistant Food Editor: Coleen Martin
Test Kitchen Home Economists: Rochelle Schmidt, Karla Spies
Test Kitchen Assistant: Judith Scholovich
Assistant Editor: Kristine Krueger
Art Director: Stephanie Marchese
Production: Ellen Lloyd
Photography: Scott Anderson
Prop Stylist: Anne Schimmel

©1995, Reiman Publications, L.P.
5400 S. 60th St., Greendale WI 53129
International Standard Book Number: 0-89821-196-4
Library of Congress Catalog Card Number: 95-67576
All rights reserved.
Printed in U.S.A.

PICTURED ON OUR COVER. Clockwise from the bottom: Chicken 'n' Peppers (page 40), Golden Chicken (page 33) and Roasted Chicken with Sausage Stuffing (page 56).

Country Chicken

Hearty Starters...4

✿✿✿✿✿✿

Garden-Fresh Salads...8

✿✿✿✿✿✿

Soups & Sandwiches...16

✿✿✿✿✿✿

Country-Fried Favorites...30

✿✿✿✿✿✿

Skillet Specialties...38

✿✿✿✿✿✿

Oven Entrees...54

✿✿✿✿✿✿

Comforting Casseroles...70

✿✿✿✿✿✿

Festive Family Fare...80

✿✿✿✿✿✿

Hot Off the Grill...86

✿✿✿✿✿✿

Index...96

Hearty Starters

These appealing hot and cold appetizers are the perfect "grand opening" for potlucks and picnics. Or serve them as a satisfying anytime snack.

Sesame Chicken with Honey Sauce

Donna Shull, Pipersville, Pennsylvania
(PICTURED AT LEFT)

Between working and raising three children, we don't have much time on our hands. These crunchy chicken bites can be prepared in a hurry for a super snack or light dinner.

- 1/2 cup fine dry bread crumbs
- 1/4 cup sesame seeds
- 1/2 cup mayonnaise
- 1 teaspoon dry mustard
- 1 teaspoon dried minced onion
- 3 boneless skinless chicken breast halves, cooked and cubed (4 cups)

SAUCE:
- 1/2 cup mayonnaise
- 1/4 cup honey

In a plastic bag, mix bread crumbs and sesame seeds; set aside. In a small bowl, combine mayonnaise, mustard and onion. Coat chicken pieces with mayonnaise mixture, then toss in crumb mixture. Place on a greased baking sheet. Bake at 425° for 10-12 minutes or until lightly browned. Combine sauce ingredients; serve with the hot chicken. **Yield:** 6-8 servings.

Teriyaki Chicken Wings

Anita Ocampo, Mandan, North Dakota
(PICTURED AT LEFT)

When my sister-in-law served these at a family party years ago, we all kept reaching for "just one more". I often prepare them for our toddler son...it's the only way I can get him to eat chicken!

- 3 pounds whole chicken wings
- 1 cup all-purpose flour
- 1-1/2 teaspoons garlic powder
- 1 teaspoon salt
- 1/2 teaspoon pepper
- Cooking oil for deep-fat frying
- 3/4 cup soy sauce
- 3/4 cup sugar

Cut chicken wings into three sections; discard wing tip section. In a large bowl or plastic bag, combine flour, garlic powder, salt and pepper. Add wings; toss to coat. In an electric skillet or deep-fat fryer, heat oil to 350°. Fry chicken wings, a few at a time, for about 9 minutes or until juices run clear. Drain on paper towels. In a saucepan,

combine soy sauce and sugar; cook and stir until sugar dissolves, about 5 minutes. Dip fried wings briefly in sauce; serve immediately. **Yield:** 12-14 servings.

Tex-Mex Dip

Cyndi Reason, Ruidoso, New Mexico
(PICTURED AT LEFT)

Here in the Southwest, we enjoy Mexican food. And this delicious dip always gets rave reviews...no matter how often I make it. Everyone loves the great combination of chicken, bean dip and assorted toppings.

- 1 can (10-1/2 ounces) bean dip
- 3/4 cup sour cream
- 2 tablespoons taco seasoning
- 1 can (2-1/2 ounces) sliced ripe olives, drained
- 1 cup finely chopped cooked chicken
- 1 medium tomato, seeded and diced
- 1 green onion, sliced
- 1 cup (4 ounces) shredded cheddar cheese

Tortilla chips

Spread bean dip evenly on a 10-in. to 12-in. serving platter; set aside. In a small bowl, combine sour cream and taco seasoning; spread carefully over bean dip. Sprinkle with olives, chicken, tomato, onion and cheese. Cover and chill for at least 2 hours. Serve with tortilla chips. **Yield:** 6-8 servings.

Crunchy Chicken Balls

Jamie Cox, Chatham, Virginia

Now that I'm retired from teaching, I have plenty of time to entertain. These individual chicken balls are always on the menu...much to the pleasure of my guests.

✓ This tasty dish uses less sugar, salt and fat. Recipe includes *Diabetic Exchanges*.

- 1 cup finely chopped cooked chicken
- 1/4 cup minced green onions
- 1/2 cup finely shredded sharp cheddar cheese
- 1/4 teaspoon salt, optional
- 1/8 teaspoon pepper
- 2 tablespoons mayonnaise
- 3/4 cup finely chopped pecans *or* chopped fresh parsley

In a bowl, combine the first six ingredients; mix well. Shape into 3/4-in. balls. Roll in pecans or parsley. Cover and chill. **Yield:** 8 servings (2 dozen). **Diabetic Exchanges:** One serving (prepared with low-fat cheese, light mayonnaise and parsley and without added salt) equals 1 lean meat; also, 49 calories, 79 mg sodium, 16 mg cholesterol, 2 gm carbohydrate, 5 gm protein, 3 gm fat.

SOUTHWESTERN SNACKS. *Pictured at left, top to bottom: Sesame Chicken with Honey Sauce, Teriyaki Chicken Wings and Tex-Mex Dip (all recipes on this page).*

Curried Chicken Cheese Ball
Pauline Rhine, Bunker Hill, Indiana

I cater for parties and weddings, so I'm always searching for new menu ideas. I found a similar cheese ball recipe in a magazine, then adjusted the ingredients to suit my tastes.

✓ **This tasty dish uses less sugar, salt and fat. Recipe includes** *Diabetic Exchanges.*

   1 package (8 ounces) cream cheese, softened
   2 tablespoons orange marmalade
1-1/2 teaspoons curry powder
 1/2 teaspoon salt, optional
 1/4 teaspoon white pepper
   2 cups finely chopped cooked chicken
   2 tablespoons minced green onions
   2 tablespoons minced celery
 3/4 cup chopped toasted almonds *or* chopped fresh parsley
Crackers

In a mixing bowl, beat cream cheese, marmalade, curry powder, salt if desired and pepper until smooth. Stir in chicken, onions and celery. Shape into a large ball. Roll in almonds or parsley. Cover and chill. Serve with crackers. **Yield:** 10 servings (2 cups). **Diabetic Exchanges:** One 3-tablespoon serving (prepared with light cream cheese and parsley and without added salt) equals 1/2 meat, 1/2 fat, 1/2 fruit; also, 89 calories, 135 mg sodium, 30 mg cholesterol, 5 gm carbohydrate, 7 gm protein, 5 gm fat.

Smoky Chicken Spread
Mary Beth Wagner, Rio, Wisconsin

The unique "smoky" flavor in this spread comes from smoked almonds. It makes a hearty snack on your favorite crackers. Don't expect many leftovers!

   3 cups finely chopped cooked chicken
 1/2 cup finely chopped celery
 1/2 cup coarsely chopped smoked almonds
 3/4 cup mayonnaise
 1/4 cup finely chopped onion
   1 tablespoon honey
 1/2 teaspoon seasoned salt
 1/8 teaspoon pepper
Crackers

In a bowl, combine the first eight ingredients; mix well. Cover and chill at least 2 hours. Serve with crackers. **Yield:** 16-20 servings (4 cups).

Hot Wings
Dawn Wright, Moline, Michigan

You'll find these wings have just the right amount of "zip". But if you want them a little hotter—like we often do—simply add more hot pepper sauce. I hope you enjoy them!

   4 pounds whole chicken wings

     Cooking oil for deep-fat frying
 1/4 cup butter *or* margarine
 1/4 cup honey
 1/4 cup barbecue sauce
   4 to 6 tablespoons hot pepper sauce
   3 tablespoons vinegar
   3 tablespoons prepared mustard
 1/4 teaspoon garlic salt
Celery and carrot sticks
Blue cheese *or* ranch salad dressing

Cut wings into three sections; discard wing tip section. In an electric skillet or deep-fat fryer, heat oil to 350°. Fry chicken wings, a few at a time, about 9 minutes or until golden. Drain on paper towels; place in a large bowl. In a saucepan, combine the next seven ingredients; cook and stir 5-10 minutes. Pour over cooked wings; let stand 10 minutes. With a slotted spoon, remove wings from sauce and place in a single layer on greased baking sheets. Bake at 350° for 15 minutes. Serve hot with vegetable sticks and dressing for dipping. **Yield:** 12-16 servings.

Cheesy Pecan Roll
Angie Monk, Quitman, Texas

Years ago, I judged a local 4-H Food Show, where this cheese roll won first prize in the snack foods category. My family has also labeled it a winner!

   1 package (8 ounces) cream cheese, softened
   2 teaspoons steak sauce
 1/2 teaspoon salt
 1/4 teaspoon garlic powder
 3/4 cup finely chopped cooked chicken
   2 tablespoons minced celery
   1 tablespoon minced onion
 1/2 cup finely chopped toasted pecans
Crackers

In a bowl, combine cream cheese, steak sauce, salt and garlic powder until smooth. Stir in chicken, celery and onion. Shape into a 9-in.-long log. Roll in pecans. Cover and chill. Serve with crackers. **Yield:** 8-10 servings.

Aunt Shirley's Liver Pate
Shirley Brownell, Amsterdam, New York

While living in San Francisco, I developed this recipe to serve at our many get-togethers with friends. Now my nieces and nephews request my liver pate at family gatherings.

 3/4 cup butter *or* margarine, *divided*
1-1/4 pounds chicken livers, halved
 1/4 cup chopped onion
   2 teaspoons Worcestershire sauce
   1 tablespoon minced fresh parsley
 1/4 cup sliced stuffed olives
Additional parsley, optional
Crackers

In a large skillet, melt 1/2 cup butter. Add chicken livers, onion, Worcestershire sauce and parsley. Saute over medium heat for 6-8 minutes or until chicken is no longer pink. Remove from the heat; cool for 10 minutes. Transfer to a blender; process until smooth. Melt the remaining butter; cool to lukewarm. Add to blender and process until blended. Pour into a 2-1/2-cup mold that has been lined with plastic wrap. Cover and chill for 8 hours or overnight. Before serving, unmold pate onto a chilled plate. Press olives on top of pate; garnish with parsley if desired. Serve with crackers. **Yield:** 8-10 servings (2-1/4 cups).

Empanditas
Mary Ann Kosmas, Minneapolis, Minnesota

These mini chicken pockets are one of my favorite appetizers because they can be made ahead of time and frozen. So they're a perfect snack when unexpected company drops in.

- 2 boneless skinless chicken breast halves, thinly sliced
- 1 tablespoon cooking oil
- 1/8 teaspoon ground cumin
- 1 can (4 ounces) chopped green chilies, drained
- 1/2 cup shredded pepper jack *or* Monterey Jack cheese
- 2 tablespoons all-purpose flour
- Pastry for 2 double-crust pies
- 1/4 cup milk

In a large skillet, saute chicken in oil for 7-8 minutes or until juices run clear. Sprinkle with cumin. Chop into very small pieces and place in a bowl. Add chilies and cheese. Sprinkle with flour; toss to coat. Turn pastry dough onto a floured board; roll to 1/8-in. thickness. Cut with a 2-in. circle cutter. Fill each circle with about 1 tablespoon of filling. Wet edges of circle with water. Fold half of pastry over filling; seal with fingers, then press with the tines of a fork. Repeat until all filling is used. Place on a greased baking sheet. Brush lightly with milk. Bake at 375° for 20-25 minutes or until golden brown. Serve hot. **Yield:** 10-12 servings (about 3 dozen). **Editor's Note:** Empanditas may be frozen after sealing. Brush with milk and bake for 30-35 minutes.

Three-Cheese Nachos
Cari Hinz, Eau Claire, Wisconsin

I received the recipe for these tasty nachos from a co-worker a few years back. They're fun to serve as party appetizers or as the main course at a casual dinner with family.

- 2 packages (one 8 ounces, one 3 ounces) cream cheese, softened
- 1 can (4 ounces) chopped green chilies
- 3 tablespoons chopped onion
- 2 garlic cloves, minced
- 1 tablespoon canned chopped jalapeno pepper
- 1-1/2 teaspoons ground cumin
- 1-1/2 teaspoons chili powder
- 2 cups cubed cooked chicken
- 2 cups (8 ounces) shredded Monterey Jack cheese, *divided*

- 1 package (14 ounces) pita bread (6 inches)
- 1 cup (4 ounces) shredded cheddar cheese
- Salsa, optional

In a mixing bowl, beat cream cheese, chilies, onion, garlic, jalapeno, cumin and chili powder until smooth. Stir in chicken and 1 cup Monterey Jack cheese. Split each pita into two circles. Spread 1/4 cup of chicken mixture on each circle; place on ungreased baking sheets. Bake at 400 for 5-10 minutes. Mix cheddar cheese and remaining Monterey Jack; sprinkle over the circles. Bake 5 minutes longer or until cheese is melted. Cut into wedges and serve with salsa if desired. **Yield:** 10-12 servings.

Sweet-and-Sour Chicken Nuggets
Helen Boese, St. Cloud, Florida

Homemade chicken nuggets are better than any store-bought version could ever be. With the simple special sauce, these appetizers work well for special occasions and every day.

- 1/2 cup fine dry bread crumbs
- 2 teaspoons lemon-pepper seasoning
- 4 boneless skinless chicken breast halves, cubed
- 3 tablespoons cooking oil
- SAUCE:
- 2 tablespoons sugar
- 2 tablespoons ketchup
- 2 tablespoons soy sauce
- 2 tablespoons vinegar

In a bowl or plastic bag, combine bread crumbs and lemon-pepper seasoning. Add chicken pieces, a few at a time, and toss to coat. Heat oil in a skillet over medium heat. Cook and stir chicken for about 5 minutes or until juices run clear. In a small saucepan, combine sauce ingredients; stir until heated through. Serve with chicken. **Yield:** 6-8 servings.

Buttery Chicken Spread
Candice Oswald, Sidney, Michigan

I have fond memories of my grandmother preparing this rich and delicious snack. It's stood the test of time and remains a crowd-pleaser today.

- 1 package (8 ounces) cream cheese, softened
- 3 cups shredded cooked chicken
- 1 cup butter *or* margarine, softened
- 1/4 cup minced fresh parsley
- 2 tablespoons minced onion
- 1 teaspoon lemon juice
- 1/2 to 1 teaspoon dill weed
- 1/8 teaspoon salt
- Dash ground cinnamon
- Party bread, toast *or* crackers

In a bowl, combine the first nine ingredients; mix well. Transfer to a small crock or serving dish. Cover and chill at least 1 hour. Let stand at room temperature 20 minutes before serving. Serve with bread, toast or crackers. **Yield:** 20-25 servings (3-1/2 cups).

Garden-Fresh Salads

Toss aside traditional chicken salads! These extraordinary renditions are packed with refreshing fruits and vegetables and hearty rice and pasta.

Chicken Caesar Salad
Anne Frederick, New Hartford, New York
(PICTURED AT LEFT)

You'll find this salad makes a nice addition to any brunch buffet. The robust Caesar dressing adds some "zest" to the mild flavors of chicken and vegetables.

- 2 cups cooked chicken strips
- 2 anchovy fillets, finely chopped, optional
- 1/2 cup mayonnaise
- 1 tablespoon grated Parmesan cheese
- 1 tablespoon red wine vinegar
- 1 teaspoon Worcestershire sauce
- 1 teaspoon Dijon mustard
- 1 garlic clove, minced
- 1/2 large bunch romaine lettuce, torn
- 1 small red onion, sliced into rings
- 1 carrot, julienned

In a large bowl, combine the first eight ingredients. Just before serving, stir in lettuce, onion and carrot; toss to coat. **Yield:** 4 servings.

Broccoli-Cauliflower Toss
Merry McNally, Ionia, Michigan
(PICTURED AT LEFT)

My family spends a lot of time outdoors in the summer. Served with homemade bread and fresh fruit, this chicken and vegetable salad makes a light and easy meal.

- 1-1/2 cups fresh broccoli florets
- 1/2 cup fresh cauliflowerets
- 1/2 cup sliced carrots
- 1/4 cup water
- 1 cup cubed cooked chicken
- 6 cherry tomatoes, halved

DRESSING:
- 2/3 cup vegetable oil
- 1/3 cup red wine vinegar
- 2 teaspoons honey
- 1 teaspoon minced fresh basil *or* 1/4 teaspoon dried basil
- 1/2 teaspoon salt
- 1/4 teaspoon pepper

In a large covered saucepan, steam broccoli, cauliflower and carrots in water for 2-3 minutes; drain. Place in a bowl; add chicken and tomatoes. Combine dressing in-

---

MOUTH-WATERING MEDLEY. *Pictured at left, top to bottom: Chicken Caesar Salad, Broccoli-Cauliflower Toss and Brown Rice Apple Salad (all recipes on this page).*

---

gredients; pour over salad. Cover and chill for at least 4 hours, stirring occasionally. Drain before serving. **Yield:** 4 servings.

Brown Rice Apple Salad
Sue Yaeger, Brookings, South Dakota
(PICTURED AT LEFT)

When I want to serve a different type of salad, this is the recipe I frequently reach for. It meets all my "requirements" for a great recipe—fast, filling...and foolproof!

- 2 medium tart apples, cut into 1/2-inch pieces
- 1 tablespoon lemon juice
- 1 medium green *or* sweet red pepper, cut into 1/2-inch pieces
- 3 boneless skinless chicken breast halves, cooked and cut into 1/2-inch pieces
- 3-1/2 cups cooked brown rice
- 1/2 cup chopped pecans, toasted
- 1/4 cup sliced green onions
- 1/3 cup vegetable oil
- 1/4 cup chopped fresh parsley
- 3 tablespoons raspberry vinegar
- 1 teaspoon sugar
- 1/2 teaspoon salt
- 1/4 teaspoon pepper

Lettuce leaves, optional

In a large bowl, toss apples with lemon juice. Add next five ingredients; mix well and set aside. For dressing, whisk together next six ingredients until smooth; pour over salad. Chill until ready to serve. Serve on lettuce leaves if desired. **Yield:** 10 servings.

Spicy Barbecue Chicken Salad
Michele Armentrout, New Hope, Virginia

I came up with this one-of-a-kind salad as a way to use left-over barbecued chicken. People who try it have a hard time figuring out what makes it so deliciously different!

- 3 cups cubed cooked *or* barbecued chicken
- 1/2 cup chopped celery
- 1/4 cup finely chopped onion
- 1 tablespoon sweet pickle relish
- 1/2 cup mayonnaise
- 3 tablespoons barbecue sauce
- 1/4 teaspoon dry mustard
- 1/4 teaspoon hot pepper sauce

Lettuce leaves *or* hard rolls, optional

In a large bowl, toss chicken, celery, onion and relish. Combine mayonnaise, barbecue sauce, mustard and hot pepper sauce until well mixed. Stir into chicken mixture. Cover and chill until ready to serve. Serve on lettuce leaves or rolls if desired. **Yield:** 4-6 servings.

Chicken 'n' Rice Salad

Melinda Flath, Garrison, North Dakota

My duties as wife, mother and schoolteacher tend to keep me out of the kitchen. So this superbly simple salad comes in handy when dinnertime is fast approaching.

  1 package (6.9 ounces) chicken-flavored Rice-A-Roni
1-1/2 cups cubed cooked chicken
  1 cup fresh broccoli florets
  1 cup sliced celery
  1 cup mayonnaise
1/2 cup chopped green pepper
1/4 cup finely chopped onion
  1 can (8 ounces) sliced water chestnuts, drained
1/4 teaspoon salt
1/4 teaspoon pepper
Lettuce leaves, optional

Prepare rice according to package directions; cool. In a large bowl, combine all ingredients except lettuce. Cover and chill until ready to serve. Serve on lettuce leaves if desired. **Yield:** 8 servings.

Chicken Salad Supreme

Eleanor Grofvert, Kalamazoo, Michigan

Now that my husband and I are retired, we live in Florida for most of the winter. I often prepare this creamy, fruity chicken salad for a wonderful warm-weather lunch.

  5 cups cubed cooked chicken
  2 tablespoons vegetable oil
  2 tablespoons orange juice
  2 tablespoons vinegar
  1 teaspoon salt
  3 cups cooked rice
1-1/2 cups mayonnaise
1-1/2 cups sliced celery
1-1/2 cups small seedless green grapes
  1 can (20 ounces) pineapple chunks, drained
  1 can (11 ounces) mandarin oranges, drained
  1 cup slivered almonds, toasted

In a large bowl, combine chicken, oil, orange juice, vinegar and salt. Fold in rice, mayonnaise, celery, grapes, pineapple and oranges. Cover and chill until ready to serve; stir in almonds. **Yield:** 12 servings.

Black-Eyed Peas Salad

Reesa Byrd, Enterprise, Alabama

This hearty salad tastes extra-special if the flavors are allowed to blend overnight. But once my family knows I'm making their most-requested dish, it disappears quickly!

  2 cups cubed cooked chicken
  2 teaspoons seasoned salt
  1 can (15-1/2 ounces) black-eyed peas, rinsed and drained
  1 can (15 ounces) white or yellow corn, drained
  1 can (8 ounces) sliced water chestnuts, drained
  1 cup mayonnaise
  1 cup sliced celery
  1 cup cooked wild rice
3/4 cup chopped cucumber
1/2 cup fresh broccoli florets
1/2 cup chopped green pepper
1/4 teaspoon pepper

Place the chicken in a large bowl; sprinkle with seasoned salt. Add remaining ingredients and mix well. Cover and chill until ready to serve. **Yield:** 8 servings.

Greek Chicken Salad

Linda Walter, Hugoton, Kansas

Juggling work and family calls for fast, nutritious meals. So I prepare this satisfying salad frequently, particularly when garden-fresh cucumbers and parsley are abundant.

  3 cups cubed cooked chicken
  2 medium cucumbers, diced
1-1/4 cups cubed Swiss or crumbled feta cheese
2/3 cup sliced ripe olives
1/4 cup chopped fresh parsley
  1 cup mayonnaise
1/2 cup plain yogurt
  1 garlic clove, minced
1-1/2 teaspoons dried oregano
1/2 teaspoon grated lemon peel
Salt to taste
Lettuce leaves or pita bread

In a large bowl, combine chicken, cucumbers, cheese, olives and parsley. In a small bowl, combine mayonnaise, yogurt, garlic, oregano, lemon peel and salt. Pour over chicken mixture; toss lightly until coated. Cover and chill until ready to serve. Serve on lettuce leaves or in pita bread. **Yield:** 8 servings.

Tropical Fruit Medley

Jodi Cigel, Stevens Point, Wisconsin

You'll especially appreciate this salad in winter when fresh fruit isn't readily available. Serving a smaller crowd? No problem! The recipe can easily be cut in half.

  8 cups cubed cooked chicken
  3 cups sliced celery
  1 can (16 ounces) apricot halves, drained and chopped
  2 cans (16 ounces *each*) chunky mixed fruit, drained
  3 cups mayonnaise
1/2 cup French salad dressing
  3 tablespoons red wine vinegar
  2 tablespoons honey
  1 tablespoon curry powder
  1 cup chopped pecans, toasted

In a large bowl, combine chicken, celery and fruit. Combine mayonnaise, salad dressing, vinegar, honey and curry powder. Pour over chicken mixture; toss to coat. Cover and chill until ready to serve. Sprinkle with pecans. **Yield:** 20 servings.

Waldorf Salad
Joan Miner Vallem, Arroyo Grande, California

My husband and I are now retired and travel the country in our mobile home. When not taking in the beautiful sights, I'm in the kitchen preparing many new tasty dishes.

- 6 cups cubed cooked chicken
- 6 hard-cooked eggs, chopped
- 6 celery ribs, sliced
- 2 cups seedless green grapes, halved
- 2 cups diced red apples

Juice of 1 lemon
- 2 cups mayonnaise
- 2 tablespoons prepared horseradish
- 2 tablespoons Dijon mustard
- 1/2 teaspoon salt
- 1/2 teaspoon pepper
- 3/4 cup chopped pecans, toasted
- 6 cups torn lettuce

In a large bowl, combine chicken, eggs, celery and grapes. Toss apples with lemon juice; add mayonnaise, horseradish, mustard, salt and pepper. Mix well. Toss with chicken mixture until coated. Cover and chill until ready to serve. Add pecans; serve over a bed of lettuce. **Yield:** 8 servings.

Garden Party Salad
Daphne Bruce, Penfield, New York

I knew I had to add this salad to my collection as soon as I sampled it at a garden club supper. I wasn't alone…everyone asked the woman who brought it for the recipe!

- 1/4 cup vegetable oil
- 1/4 cup orange marmalade
- 3 tablespoons cider vinegar
- 3 tablespoons mayonnaise
- 2 teaspoons curry powder
- 1/4 teaspoon hot pepper sauce
- 6 cups cubed cooked chicken
- 2 tablespoons golden raisins
- 2 tablespoons slivered almonds, toasted
- 2 tablespoons minced fresh parsley

In a small bowl, whisk first six ingredients until smooth; chill. Just before serving, combine chicken, raisins, almonds and parsley in a large bowl; add dressing and toss. **Yield:** 6 servings.

Susan's Stuffed Tomatoes
Susan Kemmerer, Telford, Pennsylvania

Before I created this recipe, I wasn't much of a salad eater. Now it's a summertime specialty. Even my husband and four sons look forward to these super stuffed tomatoes.

- 2 cups finely chopped cooked chicken
- 1/2 cup mayonnaise
- 1/4 cup finely chopped celery
- 1/4 cup finely shredded cheddar cheese
- 1 small carrot, finely shredded
- 1 tablespoon finely chopped onion

- 1/4 teaspoon pepper

Salt to taste
- 5 medium tomatoes, cored

Lettuce leaves, optional

In a bowl, combine the first eight ingredients; cover and chill for 2-3 hours. Cut tomatoes not quite through into six equal wedges; spread apart. Place 1/2 cup chicken salad in center of each tomato. Serve on lettuce if desired. **Yield:** 5 servings.

Summertime Salad with Honey Dressing
Tami Harrington, Scottsdale, Arizona

There's nothing like fresh fruit to keep you cool in the summer heat. My family is delighted whenever I serve this refreshing salad. It's also a hit at potlucks.

- 4 cups cubed cooked chicken
- 1-1/2 cups fresh peach chunks (about 2 peaches)
- 1-1/2 cups fresh pineapple chunks
- 1 cup sliced fresh strawberries
- 1 cup chopped celery
- 3/4 cup slivered almonds
- 1/2 cup chopped red onion

HONEY DRESSING:
- 1 cup mayonnaise
- 3/4 cup peach preserves *or* orange marmalade
- 1 tablespoon honey
- 2 teaspoons Dijon mustard
- 1/2 teaspoon salt

In a large bowl, combine chicken, fruit, celery, almonds and onion. Mix dressing ingredients in a small bowl. Pour about 1/2 cup (just enough to moisten) over chicken mixture; toss to coat. Cover and chill salad and leftover dressing for several hours. Add remaining dressing just before serving. **Yield:** 6-8 servings.

Minnesota Wild Rice Salad
Mary Hulin, Lake Worth, Florida

Everyone thinks this is one of my best salads because it features wild rice—a major crop in my home state of Minnesota. Cashews give a subtle nutty flavor.

- 6 cups water
- 3/4 cup uncooked wild rice
- 3/4 teaspoon salt, *divided*
- 2-1/2 cups cubed cooked chicken
- 1 can (8 ounces) pineapple chunks, drained and halved
- 2 cups sliced celery
- 1-1/2 cups seedless green grapes, halved
- 3/4 cup mayonnaise
- 1/2 cup chutney
- 3/4 cup cashew pieces

In a medium saucepan, bring water to a boil. Add rice and 1/4 teaspoon salt. Cover tightly and simmer for 50 minutes. Cool; drain if necessary. In a large bowl, combine rice, chicken, pineapple, celery, grapes, mayonnaise, chutney and remaining salt. Cover and chill until ready to serve; toss with cashews. **Yield:** 8-10 servings.

Stir-Fry Spinach Salad
Victoria Schreur, Lowell, Michigan
(PICTURED AT LEFT)

I first served this at a party...it was an instant hit. I'm sure you and your family will like the slightly sweet- and-sour sauce in this unique salad.

✓ This tasty dish uses less sugar, salt and fat. Recipe includes *Diabetic Exchanges*.

- 1 can (8 ounces) pineapple chunks
- 1 pound boneless skinless chicken breasts, julienned
- 2 tablespoons cooking oil
- 1 medium green pepper, julienned
- 3 tablespoons brown sugar
- 1 tablespoon cornstarch
- 1/4 cup ketchup
- 3 tablespoons vinegar
- 2 tablespoons soy sauce
- 6 cups torn fresh spinach
- 1 cup cherry tomato halves

Drain pineapple, reserving 3 tablespoons juice in a small bowl; set pineapple aside. (Discard remaining juice or save for another use.) In a skillet or wok, stir-fry chicken in oil for 5 minutes or until no longer pink. Add green pepper; stir-fry for 2-4 minutes or until crisp-tender. Meanwhile, add brown sugar and cornstarch to pineapple juice; mix well. Stir in ketchup, vinegar and soy sauce until smooth; add to skillet and cook until thickened. On a large serving platter, arrange spinach, pineapple and tomatoes. Top with chicken and green pepper; serve immediately. **Yield:** 6 servings. **Diabetic Exchanges:** One serving (prepared with unsweetened pineapple and low-sodium soy sauce) equals 2 lean meat, 2 vegetable, 1 fruit; also, 230 calories, 480 mg sodium, 53 mg cholesterol, 22 gm carbohydrate, 21 gm protein, 8 gm fat.

Fruity Rice Salad
Lani Haveman, Sedro Woolley, Washington

Ranch dressing adds a little "zip" to this fresh, flavorful salad. It makes a great lunch or supper on a hot summer day when you feel like eating something a little less filling.

- 1/2 cup mayonnaise
- 1/2 cup ranch salad dressing
- 1 teaspoon salt
- 2-1/2 cups cubed cooked chicken
- 1-1/2 cups cooked rice
- 3/4 cup sliced celery
- 3/4 cup small green grapes
- 1/2 cup drained pineapple tidbits
- 1/2 cup drained mandarin oranges
- 1/2 cup slivered almonds, toasted

In a large bowl, combine mayonnaise, salad dressing

> **MEALS WITH APPEAL.** *Pictured at left, top to bottom: Stir-Fry Spinach Salad and Creamy Chicken Crunch (both recipes on this page).*

---

and salt. Fold in chicken, rice, celery and fruit. Cover and chill until ready to serve; add almonds. **Yield:** 4-6 servings.

Creamy Chicken Crunch
Denise Goedeken, Platte Center, Nebraska
(PICTURED AT LEFT)

Whenever I take this salad to church functions and family picnics, I always come home with an empty bowl. And as any cook knows, that's a sure sign of success!

- 1-1/2 cups cubed cooked chicken
- 1 cup frozen peas, thawed and drained
- 1/2 cup sliced celery
- 1/2 cup chopped green pepper
- 1/2 cup fresh pea pods, halved
- 1/4 cup sliced green onions
- 1 cup mayonnaise
- 2 tablespoons lemon juice
- 1 teaspoon soy sauce
- 1/4 teaspoon ground ginger
- 1 can (3 ounces) chow mein noodles (1-1/2 cups)
- 1/4 cup salted peanuts

In a large bowl, combine the first six ingredients. Stir together mayonnaise, lemon juice, soy sauce and ginger; pour over chicken mixture. Toss lightly to coat; cover and chill until ready to serve. Fold in chow mein noodles and peanuts just before serving. **Yield:** 4-6 servings.

Melon Salad with Ginger Dressing
Elsie Mauriello, Atkinson, New Hampshire

With a hint of honey, the cool, creamy dressing complements the colorful melon and tender chicken. Family and friends will be happy to see it on your table again and again.

DRESSING:
- 2/3 cup mayonnaise
- 2/3 cup sour cream
- Juice of 1 lime
- 2 teaspoons honey
- 1/2 teaspoon ground ginger
- 1/2 teaspoon salt
- 1/4 teaspoon pepper

SALAD:
- 3 boneless skinless chicken breast halves
- 1 cup apple juice
- 1 cup water
- 1 teaspoon whole black peppercorns
- 2 celery ribs, sliced
- 2 cups cantaloupe balls
- 2 cups honeydew balls
- 1/4 cup chopped fresh parsley
- Lettuce leaves, optional

In a small bowl, combine all dressing ingredients; cover and chill. In a large covered saucepan, simmer chicken in apple juice, water and peppercorns for 20 minutes or until chicken juices run clear. Discard broth; allow chicken to cool. Slice into thin strips and place in a large bowl. Add celery, melon balls and parsley. Serve on a bed of lettuce if desired. Drizzle with dressing. **Yield:** 6-8 servings.

Cheesy Pasta Salad
Sandi Green, Jackson, Michigan

This creamy pasta salad came about when I combined ingredients from two different recipes. It got rave reviews when I served it at a baby shower.

- 4 cups cubed cooked chicken
- 1 package (8 ounces) spiral pasta, cooked, drained and cooled
- 1-1/2 cups cubed Gouda *or* Monterey Jack cheese
- 1 cup sliced celery
- 1 cup seedless green grapes
- 1 cup mayonnaise
- 1/4 cup sour cream
- 3 tablespoons lemon juice
- 3 tablespoons honey
- 1 teaspoon dried thyme
- 1/2 teaspoon dry mustard
- 1/4 teaspoon white pepper
- 2/3 cup chopped pecans, toasted

Lettuce leaves, optional

In a large bowl, combine chicken, pasta, cheese, celery and grapes. In a small bowl, combine next seven ingredients. Pour over chicken mixture and toss to coat. Cover and chill until ready to serve; toss with pecans. **Yield:** 12 servings.

Overnight Chicken Fruit Salad
Judy Rugg, Fairport, New York

When planning a luncheon, I like to use recipes that can be prepared the night before. The tropical taste in this make-ahead salad appeals to the ladies...as well as the men!

- 3 cups cubed cooked chicken
- 1 pound seedless red grapes, halved
- 1 cup sliced celery
- 1 can (8 ounces) sliced water chestnuts, drained
- 1 cup mayonnaise
- 1 tablespoon soy sauce
- 1 tablespoon lemon juice
- 1 teaspoon curry powder
- 1 cup slivered almonds, toasted

In a large bowl, combine chicken, grapes, celery and water chestnuts. Combine mayonnaise, soy sauce, lemon juice and curry powder. Pour over chicken mixture; toss lightly until coated. Cover and chill 8 hours or overnight. Stir in almonds just before serving. **Yield:** 8 servings.

Fiesta Salad
Connie Bolton, San Antonio, Texas

If you're tired of the same old chicken salad, try this slightly spicy version. It's attractive and tasty, so it's perfect for every day and special occasions.

- 1 cup mayonnaise
- 1 can (4 ounces) chopped green chilies, drained
- 1 tablespoon chili powder
- 1 tablespoon lemon *or* lime juice

- 1/2 teaspoon salt
- 1/4 teaspoon hot pepper sauce
- 3-1/2 cups cooked rice, chilled
- 2 cups cubed cooked chicken
- 1 green onion, sliced
- 1/2 cup chopped green pepper

Lettuce leaves
- 1 medium tomato, chopped
- 1 medium avocado, peeled and sliced
- 1/4 cup ripe olives, sliced

Tortilla chips

In a large bowl, combine first six ingredients. Stir in rice, chicken, green onion and green pepper. Cover and chill for 1-2 hours. Serve on a lettuce-lined platter; top with tomato, avocado, olives and chips. **Yield:** 6 servings.

Orange Pasta Salad
Marjorie Fjeld, Valley City, North Dakota

The orange dressing has a fresh flavor that really complements the chicken, pasta and fruit. And toasted almonds add lots of festive crunch.

- 5 cups cubed cooked chicken
- 3 cups cooked pasta (rotini, shells *or* wheels)
- 1-1/2 cups sliced celery
- 1/2 cup sliced green onions
- 1 cup drained pineapple tidbits
- 1 can (11 ounces) mandarin oranges, drained
- 2 kiwifruit, peeled and cut into chunks
- 1 cup mayonnaise
- 1/3 cup vegetable oil
- 2 tablespoons cider vinegar
- 2 tablespoons orange juice concentrate
- 1-1/2 teaspoons salt
- 1 teaspoon dry mustard
- 1 cup slivered almonds, toasted

In a large bowl, combine chicken, pasta, celery, onions, pineapple, oranges and kiwi. In a small bowl, mix the next six ingredients. Pour over chicken mixture; toss to coat. Cover and chill for several hours. Toss with almonds just before serving. **Yield:** 8-10 servings.

Tarragon Chicken Salad
Donna Shull, Pipersville, Pennsylvania

I clipped this recipe from the newspaper years ago. Packed with chicken and grapes, it's a hearty salad that's bound to become a favorite in your family.

- 3 cups cubed cooked chicken
- 1 cup seedless red grapes, halved
- 3/4 cup mayonnaise
- 3 tablespoons chopped fresh parsley
- 2 tablespoons milk
- 1 tablespoon tarragon vinegar
- 1 teaspoon dried tarragon
- 1/4 teaspoon pepper

Salt to taste
Lettuce *or* hollowed pineapple halves, optional
- 1/3 cup slivered almonds, toasted

In a large bowl, combine chicken and grapes. Combine the next seven ingredients. Pour over chicken mixture; toss to coat. Cover and chill at least 30 minutes. Serve on lettuce leaves or in pineapple shells if desired. Sprinkle with almonds. **Yield:** 4-6 servings.

Grilled Chicken Salad
Virginia Pugh Moon, Harvest, Alabama

Finding foods that my husband will eat is sometimes a challenge. I came up with this salad in an effort to duplicate one of his favorite restaurant dishes. He ate every bite!

✓ This tasty dish uses less sugar, salt and fat. Recipe includes *Diabetic Exchanges.*

- 1 can (8 ounces) pineapple tidbits
- 3 tablespoons soy sauce
- 1 tablespoon Worcestershire sauce
- 1/2 teaspoon garlic powder
- 1/4 to 1/2 teaspoon pepper
- 2 pounds boneless skinless chicken breasts, julienned
- 8 cups torn salad greens
- 2 large tomatoes, chopped
- 4 green onions, sliced
- Vinegar and oil salad dressing, optional

Drain pineapple, reserving juice; set pineapple aside. In a glass bowl, combine juice, soy sauce, Worcestershire sauce, garlic powder and pepper. Add chicken strips; toss to coat. Cover and chill for 2-6 hours. Grill or broil chicken strips, turning to brown both sides, for 8-10 minutes or until juices run clear. To serve, line four plates with greens; arrange tomatoes, onions, pineapple and warm chicken over greens. Drizzle with dressing if desired. **Yield:** 4 servings. **Diabetic Exchanges:** One serving (prepared with low-sodium soy sauce and served without dressing) equals 6 lean meat, 1 vegetable, 1/2 fruit; also, 383 calories, 381 mg sodium, 159 mg cholesterol, 17 gm carbohydrate, 58 gm protein, 9 gm fat.

Lemony Chicken Salad
Joan Gatling, Bernalillo, New Mexico

Every busy cook will appreciate the convenience of being able to prepare this refreshing salad ahead of time. And your family will enjoy a marvelous meal!

- 1/3 cup mayonnaise *or* salad dressing
- 1/3 cup sour cream
- 1-1/2 teaspoons fresh lemon juice
- 3/4 teaspoon grated lemon peel
- 1/2 teaspoon salt
- 1/4 teaspoon dried tarragon
- 1/8 teaspoon pepper
- 2 cups diced cooked chicken
- 1/2 cup thinly sliced celery
- 1/2 cup chopped green pepper
- 1 large red apple, cut into 1/2-inch pieces
- 1/4 cup chopped onion
- 2 tablespoons minced fresh parsley
- 1/2 cup chopped walnuts

In a large bowl, combine the first seven ingredients. Stir in chicken, celery, green pepper, apple, onion and parsley. Cover and chill for several hours. Stir in walnuts just before serving. **Yield:** 4 servings.

Almond-Apricot Chicken Salad
Susan Voigt, Plymouth, Minnesota

Here's a one-of-a-kind pasta salad that combines tender chicken, sweet apricots and crunchy vegetables. Plus, the lemony dressing can't be beat.

- 1 package (8 ounces) spiral pasta
- 1 package (6 ounces) dried apricots, thinly sliced
- 3 cups coarsely chopped fresh broccoli
- 2-1/2 cups diced cooked chicken
- 1/2 cup chopped green onions
- 1/2 cup chopped celery
- 1 cup (8 ounces) sour cream
- 3/4 cup mayonnaise
- 1 tablespoon fresh lemon juice
- 2 teaspoons grated lemon peel
- 2 teaspoons Dijon mustard
- 1-1/2 teaspoons salt
- 3/4 teaspoon dried savory
- 1/2 teaspoon pepper
- 3/4 cup sliced almonds, toasted

Cook pasta according to package directions, adding apricots during the last 4 minutes. Drain and rinse with cold water; place in a large bowl. Add broccoli, chicken, onions and celery. In a small bowl, combine the next eight ingredients. Pour over salad and toss to coat. Cover and chill until ready to serve; fold in almonds. **Yield:** 8-10 servings.

Southern-Style Chicken Salad
Marion Greer, Ballston Lake, New York

A home economics teacher from Virginia gave me the recipe for this popular sweet and tangy salad. It's a hit at gatherings here in the Northeast.

- 2 egg yolks
- 1/4 cup sugar
- 1/4 cup cider vinegar
- 2 teaspoons prepared mustard
- 1/2 teaspoon salt
- 2 tablespoons butter *or* margarine
- 2 tablespoons milk
- 2 tablespoons mayonnaise *or* salad dressing
- 4 cups diced cooked chicken
- 1-1/2 cups diced celery
- 3 hard-cooked eggs, chopped
- 2 tablespoons finely chopped onion

In a small saucepan, whisk egg yolks; add sugar, vinegar, mustard and salt. Cook over low heat, stirring constantly, until mixture thickens. Stir in butter until melted. Cover and chill for 30 minutes. Add milk and mayonnaise; mix well. In a large bowl, combine remaining ingredients. Add dressing and mix to coat. Chill until ready to serve. **Yield:** 8-10 servings.

Soups & Sandwiches

You'll put a lot of stock in these hearty soups and sandwiches! Whether served together or alone, they make a marvelous lunch or dinner.

Barbecued Chicken Sandwiches

Roberta Brown, Waupaca, Wisconsin
(PICTURED AT LEFT)

These sandwiches are great for large gatherings. The chicken can be cooked ahead of time, then added to the homemade barbecue sauce for simmering hours before guests arrive.

- 2 broiler-fryer chickens (3 to 3-1/2 pounds *each*), cooked and shredded
- 1 large onion, chopped
- 2 cups water
- 1-1/4 cups ketchup
- 1/4 cup packed brown sugar
- 1/4 cup Worcestershire sauce
- 1/4 cup red wine vinegar
- 1 teaspoon *each* salt, celery seed and chili powder
- 1/4 teaspoon hot pepper sauce
- Hamburger buns

In a 3-qt. slow cooker or Dutch oven, combine all ingredients except buns; mix well. Cook on low for 6-8 hours in the slow cooker or simmer for 1-1/2 hours on the stovetop. Serve on buns. **Yield:** 8-10 servings. **Editor's Note:** 6 cups diced cooked chicken may be used instead of the shredded chicken.

Harvest Chicken Rice Soup

Diane Winningham, Uniontown, Missouri

Because the produce in this soup is pureed, you can easily get children to eat their vegetables...without them knowing it! Kids of all ages will surely savor this classic soup.

✓ This tasty dish uses less sugar, salt and fat. Recipe includes *Diabetic Exchanges*.

- 2 celery ribs with leaves
- 2 medium carrots
- 1 pound white potatoes, peeled
- 1 pound sweet potatoes, peeled
- 3 quarts water
- 2 pounds broiler-fryer chicken pieces, skin removed
- 2 large onions, halved
- 3 chicken bouillon cubes
- 3 cups cooked rice
- Pepper to taste

Cut vegetables into 2-in. pieces; place in a 5-qt. Dutch oven. Add water, chicken, onions and bouillon. Bring to a boil; skim fat. Reduce heat; cover and simmer for 2 hours. Remove from the heat. Remove chicken and allow both broth and chicken to cool to lukewarm; skim fat. Puree the vegetables and broth in a blender; strain. Debone chicken and cut into chunks. Return chicken and broth to Dutch oven. Stir in rice. Cook over medium heat until bubbly, stirring occasionally. Season with pepper. **Yield:** 20 servings (5 quarts). **Diabetic Exchanges:** One 1-cup serving (prepared with low-sodium bouillon and rice cooked without added salt) equals 1-1/2 lean meat, 1 starch, 1 vegetable; also, 174 calories, 57 mg sodium, 41 mg cholesterol, 19 gm carbohydrate, 15 gm protein, 4 gm fat.

Chicken Soup with Stuffed Noodles

Jennifer Bucholtz, Kitchener, Ontario
(PICTURED AT LEFT)

Before retiring, I worked as a cook for 15 years. Now I spend lots of time in my kitchen preparing new, interesting food for the family. You'll love this rich homey soup.

- 1 broiler-fryer chicken (3 to 3-1/2 pounds), cut up
- 2-1/2 quarts water
- 2 teaspoons salt
- 1/4 teaspoon pepper
- 4 medium carrots, sliced
- 2 celery ribs, sliced
- 1 medium onion, diced

NOODLES:
- 1-1/4 cups all-purpose flour
- 1 teaspoon salt
- 1 egg
- 5 tablespoons water
- 1 teaspoon vegetable oil

FILLING:
- 2 eggs
- 1-1/4 cups seasoned bread crumbs
- 3 tablespoons butter *or* margarine, melted

Place chicken, water, salt and pepper in a large soup kettle. Cover and bring to a boil; skim fat. Reduce heat; cover and simmer 1-1/2 hours or until chicken is tender. Remove chicken; allow to cool. Add vegetables to broth; cook until tender. Debone chicken and cut into chunks; return to broth. Meanwhile, for noodles, mix flour and salt in a medium bowl. Make a well in the center. Beat together the egg, water and oil; pour into well. Stir together, forming a dough. Turn dough onto a floured surface; knead 8-10 times. Roll into a 16-in. x 12-in. rectangle. Combine filling ingredients; mix well. Sprinkle over dough to within 1/2 in. of edge; pat down. Moisten edges with water. Roll up jelly-roll style from long end; cut into 1/2-in. slices. Add noodles to gently boiling soup and cook for 6-8 minutes or until tender. **Yield:** 10 servings (2-1/2 quarts).

CLASSIC COMBINATION. *Pictured at left: Barbecued Chicken Sandwiches and Chicken Soup with Stuffed Noodles (both recipes on this page).*

Veggie Chicken Chili
Lois Leininger, Grants Pass, Oregon

Because this chili freezes well, I like to keep some on hand for dinner on busy days or for last-minute entertaining.

✓ **This tasty dish uses less sugar, salt and fat. Recipe includes** *Diabetic Exchanges.*

- 2 tablespoons cooking oil
- 4 cups chopped fresh broccoli
- 1 large leek *or* 4 green onions (white part only), chopped
- 1 medium red onion, chopped
- 1 medium sweet red pepper, chopped
- 1 medium green pepper, chopped
- 1 large carrot, chopped
- 2/3 cup chopped celery
- 3 garlic cloves, minced
- 4 cups chicken broth
- 4 cups cubed cooked chicken
- 2 cans (16 ounces *each*) kidney beans, rinsed and drained
- 1 can (28 ounces) diced tomatoes with liquid
- 1 can (4 ounces) chopped green chilies
- 1/4 cup packed brown sugar
- 2 tablespoons *each* ground cumin, ground coriander and dried oregano
- 2 tablespoons Worcestershire sauce
- 1 teaspoon salt, optional
- 1 cup dry white wine *or* additional chicken broth
- 1/2 cup cornstarch
- 3 tablespoons chili powder

In an 8-qt. soup kettle, heat oil. Add next eight ingredients; mix well. Cover and cook over medium-low heat for 15 minutes or until vegetables are slightly softened. Add broth, chicken, beans, tomatoes, chilies, brown sugar, cumin, coriander, oregano, Worcestershire sauce and salt if desired. Bring to a boil; reduce heat. Cover and simmer for 1 hour, stirring occasionally. Combine wine or broth, cornstarch and chili powder; stir into chili. Cook and stir until thickened. **Yield:** 20 servings (5 quarts). **Diabetic Exchanges:** One 1-cup serving (prepared with low-sodium broth and tomatoes and without added salt) equals 1 starch, 1 lean meat, 1 vegetable; also, 138 calories, 121 mg sodium, 17 mg cholesterol, 19 gm carbohydrate, 11 gm protein, 3 gm fat.

Smoked Sausage Soup
Rachel Lyn Grasmick, Rocky Ford, Colorado

This rich soup is packed with vegetables, sausage and chicken. I guarantee it's unlike any other soup you've ever tasted.

- 2 cups chopped onion
- 2 tablespoons butter *or* margarine
- 2 cups cubed cooked chicken
- 1 pound cooked smoked sausage, cut into bite-size pieces
- 3 cups sliced celery
- 3 cups sliced summer squash
- 2 cups chicken broth
- 1-1/2 cups minced fresh parsley

- 1 can (8 ounces) tomato sauce
- 2 tablespoons cornstarch
- 2 tablespoons poultry seasoning
- 1 teaspoon dried oregano
- 1 teaspoon ground cumin
- 1 teaspoon liquid smoke, optional
- 1/2 teaspoon pepper

In a skillet or microwave, cook onion in butter until softened. Transfer to a 3-qt. or larger slow cooker. Add remaining ingredients, stirring to blend. Cook on high for 5-8 hours. **Yield:** 6-8 servings (2-1/2 quarts). **Editor's Note:** The stew may also be cooked in a Dutch oven on the stovetop. Cover and simmer for 1-1/2 hours.

Chicken Broccoli Chowder
Murri Mills, Brady, Texas

I created this chowder after trying a similar version years ago. Oats give it a nice thick texture, and the blend of seasonings is absolutely wonderful.

- 2 cups sliced carrots
- 2 cups water
- 3/4 pound fresh broccoli, chopped
- 1-1/2 cups cubed cooked chicken
- 1 can (10-1/2 ounces) condensed chicken broth
- 1/2 cup chopped onion
- 1 teaspoon salt
- 1 teaspoon dried thyme
- 1/4 teaspoon garlic powder
- 1/4 teaspoon pepper
- 1 cup old-fashioned oats
- 2-1/4 cups milk

In a 3-qt. saucepan, combine the first 10 ingredients; bring to a boil. Reduce heat; cover and simmer for 15 minutes. Uncover and return to a boil. Process oats in a blender or food processor until ground; gradually stir into soup. Stir in milk. Simmer for 10 minutes, stirring constantly. Remove from the heat. Cover and let stand for 3-5 minutes before serving. **Yield:** 8 servings (2 quarts).

White Chili
Lana Rutledge, Shepherdsville, Kentucky

This chili simmers all day in a slow cooker. So when your hungry clan calls for dinner, you can ladle up steaming bowlfuls in a hurry.

✓ **This tasty dish uses less sugar, salt and fat. Recipe includes** *Diabetic Exchanges.*

- 2 medium onions, chopped
- 4 garlic cloves, minced
- 2 quarts water
- 3 pounds chicken breasts *or* thighs, skin removed
- 1 pound dry navy beans
- 2 cans (4 ounces *each*) chopped green chilies
- 1 tablespoon ground cumin
- 2 teaspoons dried oregano
- 1 teaspoon salt, optional
- 1/2 to 1 teaspoon cayenne pepper
- 1/2 teaspoon ground cloves

2 chicken bouillon cubes
Shredded Monterey Jack cheese, optional
Sour cream, optional
Dried chives and crushed red pepper flakes

Place the onions and garlic in the bottom of a slow cooker. Add the next 10 ingredients; do not stir. Cook on high for 8-10 hours. Uncover and stir (the meat should fall off the bones). Remove bones. Stir to break up the meat. Spoon into bowls; top with cheese and sour cream if desired, and sprinkle with chives and red pepper flakes. **Yield:** 12 servings (3 quarts). **Diabetic Exchanges:** One 1-cup serving (prepared with chicken breasts and low-sodium bouillon and without added salt, cheese or sour cream) equals 3 lean meat, 2 starch; also, 294 calories, 239 mg sodium, 73 mg cholesterol, 28 gm carbohydrate, 37 gm protein, 4 gm fat.

Chicken Burgers
Myrna Huebert, Tofield, Alberta

I love to cook and rarely work from any recipes. My family always wonders what's cooking in the kitchen! They really enjoy these herb-flavored chicken burgers.

1/2 cup chopped onion
3 tablespoons cooking oil, *divided*
1-1/2 pounds cooked chicken, ground *or* finely chopped
1-1/2 cups dry bread crumbs
1/2 cup grated Parmesan cheese
3 eggs
2 tablespoons dried parsley flakes
1 teaspoon *each* poultry seasoning, dried thyme, dry mustard and salt
1/2 teaspoon rubbed sage
1/2 teaspoon pepper
3/4 to 1 cup milk
8 hamburger rolls, split
Lettuce leaves
Sliced tomatoes

In a large skillet, saute onion in 1 tablespoon oil until tender. Place in a large bowl. Add chicken, crumbs, Parmesan, eggs, herbs and seasonings; mix well. Stir in enough milk to be able to shape mixture into patties. Shape into eight patties. In the same skillet, cook patties in remaining oil for 5 minutes or until browned on each side and heated through. Serve on rolls with lettuce and tomatoes. **Yield:** 8 servings.

Mom's Tomato Vegetable Soup
Sandra Davis, Brownsville, Tennessee

I developed this vegetable-based soup from a recipe my mom made when I was a child. Its robust down-home taste brings back wonderful memories of growing up on the farm.

✓ This tasty dish uses less sugar, salt and fat. Recipe includes *Diabetic Exchanges*.

1 broiler-fryer chicken (3 to 3-1/2 pounds), cut up
8 cups water
1 celery rib, halved

1 medium onion, halved
3 medium potatoes, peeled and cut into 1/2-inch cubes
2 cups tomato juice
1 can (16 ounces) mixed vegetables, drained
1 can (15-1/2 ounces) black-eyed peas, rinsed and drained
1 can (14-1/2 ounces) stewed tomatoes
1/2 cup chopped onion
2-1/2 teaspoons salt, optional
1 teaspoon pepper
1/2 pound lean ground beef
1 can (15 ounces) cream-style corn

In an 8-qt. soup kettle, place chicken, water, celery and onion. Cover and bring to a boil; skim fat. Reduce heat; cover and simmer for 1-1/2 hours or until chicken falls off the bones. Strain broth and skim fat; return broth to kettle. Add the next eight ingredients. Debone chicken and cut into chunks; return to kettle. Bring to a boil. Meanwhile, in a medium skillet, brown beef; drain and add to soup. Reduce heat; cover and simmer for 1 hour. Stir in corn; cook, uncovered, for 30 minutes, stirring occasionally. **Yield:** 18 servings (4-1/2 quarts). **Diabetic Exchanges:** One 1-cup serving (prepared with low-sodium tomato juice and tomatoes and without added salt) equals 1 meat, 1 vegetable, 1/2 starch; also, 155 calories, 69 mg sodium, 31 mg cholesterol, 15 gm carbohydrate, 14 gm protein, 4 gm fat.

Cheesy Tortilla Soup
LaVonda Owen, Marlow, Oklahoma

My daughter came up with this dish when trying to duplicate a soup she sampled at a restaurant. I always pass on to her the rave reviews I receive whenever this is served.

1 envelope chicken fajita marinade mix
4 boneless skinless chicken breast halves, diced
2 tablespoons cooking oil
1/2 cup chopped onion
1/4 cup butter *or* margarine
1/3 cup all-purpose flour
2 cans (14-1/2 ounces *each*) chicken broth
1/3 cup canned diced tomatoes with chilies
1 cup cubed process American cheese
1-1/2 cups (6 ounces) shredded Monterey Jack cheese, *divided*
1-1/2 cups half-and-half cream
Guacamole
1/2 cup shredded cheddar cheese
Tortilla chips

Prepare fajita mix according to package directions; add chicken and marinate as directed. In a medium skillet, cook chicken in oil until juices run clear; set aside. In a 3-qt. saucepan, cook onion in butter until tender. Stir in flour and cook for 1 minute. Stir in broth; cook and stir until thickened and bubbly. Add tomatoes, American cheese and 1 cup Monterey Jack; cook and stir until cheese melts. Stir in cream and chicken; heat through but do not boil. Spoon into bowls. Garnish with guacamole, cheddar cheese, remaining Monterey Jack and tortilla chips. **Yield:** 8 servings (2 quarts).

SAVOR THE FLAVOR. *Clockwise from top left: Southwestern Corn Chowder, Chicken Chili, Teriyaki Chicken Sandwiches, Chunky Chicken Soup and Curried Chicken Turnovers (all recipes on pages 22 and 23).*

Teriyaki Chicken Sandwiches

Opal Reed, Tyler, Texas
(PICTURED ON PAGE 21)

After trying a similar sandwich in Hawaii, I was inspired to create my own. My sister-in-law contributed the marinade and together we came up with this hearty version.

- 1/2 cup vegetable oil
- 1/4 cup soy sauce
- 3 tablespoons honey
- 2 tablespoons white wine vinegar
- 1 teaspoon ground ginger
- 3/4 teaspoon garlic powder
- 4 boneless skinless chicken breast halves (about 1-1/2 pounds)
- 4 hard rolls *or* croissants
- 1 cup finely shredded lettuce
- 8 tomato slices
- 4 green pepper rings
- 1/4 cup mayonnaise, optional

Combine the first six ingredients in a blender; process for 30 seconds. Reserve 1/4 cup. Pour remaining sauce into a large resealable plastic bag. Add chicken; seal and refrigerate overnight. Drain, discarding marinade. Broil chicken 4 in. from the heat for 5 minutes per side or until juices run clear. On bottom half of each roll or croissant, layer lettuce, tomatoes, chicken and green pepper. Drizzle with reserved sauce; spread with mayonnaise if desired. Top with other half of roll or croissant. **Yield:** 4 servings. **Editor's Note:** Chicken may be grilled, covered, over low coals for 10-12 minutes or until juices run clear.

Southwestern Corn Chowder

Nancy Winters, Moorpark, California
(PICTURED ON PAGE 20)

A family friend gave me this spicy chowder recipe years ago. We usually take a batch along when we go camping. It's a fast filling meal that satisfies all appetites.

- 4 boneless skinless chicken breast halves, cut into 3/4-inch cubes
- 1 medium onion, cut into thin wedges
- 1 tablespoon cooking oil
- 2 teaspoons ground cumin
- 2 cans (14-1/2 ounces *each*) chicken broth
- 1 package (10 ounces) frozen whole kernel corn
- 3/4 cup picante sauce
- 1/2 cup chopped sweet red pepper
- 1/2 cup chopped green pepper
- 2 tablespoons finely chopped fresh cilantro *or* parsley
- 2 tablespoons cornstarch
- 2 tablespoons water
- Shredded Monterey Jack cheese, optional

In a 3-qt. saucepan, cook chicken and onion in oil until chicken juices run clear. Stir in cumin. Add broth, corn and picante sauce; bring to a boil. Reduce heat; cover and simmer for 15 minutes. Stir in peppers and cilantro or parsley. Combine cornstarch and water; stir into soup.

Bring to a boil. Cook, stirring constantly, for 3 minutes or until slightly thickened. Spoon into bowls; top with cheese if desired. **Yield:** 6 servings (about 2 quarts).

Chicken Chili

Janne Rowe, Wichita, Kansas
(PICTURED ON PAGE 21)

This unique and delicious chicken chili is a much-requested meal around our house. I think you'll find it's a nice change of pace from the typical beef version.

✓ This tasty dish uses less sugar, salt and fat. Recipe includes *Diabetic Exchanges*.

- 3 cups chopped onion
- 1-1/2 cups chopped green pepper
- 4 garlic cloves, minced
- 2 tablespoons cooking oil
- 1-1/2 pounds boneless skinless chicken breasts, cut into 1/2-inch cubes
- 2 to 4 tablespoons chili powder
- 1 tablespoon ground cumin
- 2 teaspoons ground coriander
- 1/2 teaspoon cayenne pepper
- 1/2 teaspoon salt, optional
- 2 cans (14-1/2 ounces *each*) diced tomatoes with liquid
- 2 cans (10-1/2 ounces *each*) condensed chicken broth
- 2 cups water
- 1 can (6 ounces) tomato paste
- 1 bay leaf
- 2 cans (15 ounces *each*) garbanzo beans, rinsed and drained

In a 5-qt. Dutch oven, cook onion, green pepper and garlic in oil over medium-high heat for 10 minutes or until onion is tender. Add chicken; cook and stir constantly for 4 minutes or until browned. Add the next 10 ingredients; bring to a boil. Reduce heat; cover and simmer, stirring occasionally, for 40 minutes. Add beans; cook, uncovered, for 20 minutes, stirring occasionally. Remove bay leaf. **Yield:** 14 servings (3-1/2 quarts). **Diabetic Exchanges:** One 1-cup serving (prepared with low-sodium tomatoes and broth and without added salt) equals 2 lean meat, 1 starch, 1 vegetable; also, 222 calories, 230 mg sodium, 49 mg cholesterol, 26 gm carbohydrate, 18 gm protein, 6 gm fat.

Curried Chicken Turnovers

Laverne Kohut, Manning, Alberta
(PICTURED ON PAGE 20)

Whenever I have leftover chicken, I prepare plenty of these tasty turnovers and freeze them. They make a fast and flavorful meal whenever my clan's craving a chicken dish.

- 1 cup finely chopped cooked chicken
- 1 medium apple, peeled and finely chopped
- 1/2 cup mayonnaise
- 1/4 cup chopped nuts
- 1 green onion, minced
- 1 to 2 teaspoons curry powder
- 1/4 teaspoon salt

1/4 teaspoon pepper
Pastry for double-crust pie
1 egg, beaten

In a medium bowl, combine the first eight ingredients; mix well and set aside. Roll pastry to 1/8-in. thickness. Cut into 5-in. circles. Spoon about 1/4 cup filling in the center of each circle. Moisten edges of pastry with water. Fold over and seal edges with a fork. Place on a greased baking sheet. Cut 1/2-in. vents in tops. Brush with egg. Bake at 425° for 15-20 minutes or until golden brown. **Yield:** 8 servings.

Hot Chicken Heroes
Holly Jean VeDepo, West Liberty, Iowa

My mom would make these sandwiches while I was growing up. Now I make them for my own children. For variety, I sometimes substitute tuna or ham for the chicken.

    2 cups cubed cooked chicken
    1/2 cup cubed process American cheese
    1/2 cup chopped onion
    1/2 cup mayonnaise
    1/4 cup chopped green pepper
    1/4 teaspoon salt
    1/4 teaspoon pepper
    4 submarine rolls (6 inches)

In a medium bowl, combine the first seven ingredients; mix well. Spread on rolls; wrap each in heavy-duty foil and bake at 325° for 20 minutes. **Yield:** 4 servings.

Tomato Barley Soup
Jeannine Fournier, Concord, Vermont

I frequently serve this attractive soup as a mouth-watering meal after a day of skiing and sledding. Everyone who samples it comments on the robust tomato taste.

✓ This tasty dish uses less sugar, salt and fat. Recipe includes *Diabetic Exchanges*.

4-1/2 to 5 pounds broiler-fryer chicken pieces, skin
        removed
    4 quarts water
    6 large carrots, sliced
    5 medium onions, chopped
    2 cups sliced celery
    1 tablespoon minced fresh parsley
    2 teaspoons dried rosemary, crushed
    2 teaspoons salt, optional
1-1/2 teaspoons dried thyme
1-1/2 teaspoons dried savory
    1/2 teaspoon pepper
    1 cup uncooked brown rice
    1/2 cup pearl barley
    1 bottle (32 ounces) tomato juice
    1 can (28 ounces) crushed tomatoes

In an 8-qt. soup kettle, combine the first 11 ingredients. Cover and bring to a boil. Reduce heat; simmer for 2 hours. Remove chicken; allow to cool. Skim fat from broth. Debone chicken and cut into chunks; return to kettle. Add remaining ingredients; bring to a boil. Reduce heat; cover and simmer for 1 hour or until barley and rice are tender.

Yield: 28 servings (7 quarts). **Diabetic Exchanges:** One 1-cup serving (prepared with low-sodium tomato juice and without added salt) equals 1 lean meat, 1 vegetable, 1/2 starch; also, 105 calories, 110 mg sodium, 21 mg cholesterol, 14 gm carbohydrate, 9 gm protein, 2 gm fat.

Chunky Chicken Soup
Kathy Both, Rocky Mountain House, Alberta
(PICTURED ON PAGE 21)

Here's a satisfying soup that you'll find yourself serving year-round. Every spoonful is loaded with the fantastic flavor of chicken, celery, carrots and peas.

✓ This tasty dish uses less sugar, salt and fat. Recipe includes *Diabetic Exchanges*.

    3 boneless skinless chicken thighs, cut into
        1-inch pieces
    1 cup sliced celery
    1/2 cup chopped onion
    2 tablespoons cooking oil
    6 cups chicken broth
1-1/2 cups sliced carrots
    1 teaspoon dried thyme
    1/2 teaspoon salt, optional
    1/4 teaspoon pepper
    1/2 cup uncooked macaroni
1-1/2 cups frozen peas

In a 3-qt. saucepan, cook chicken, celery and onion in oil until chicken juices run clear. Add broth, carrots, thyme, salt if desired and pepper; bring to a boil. Reduce heat; cover and simmer for 45 minutes or until vegetables are tender. Stir in macaroni and peas. Cover and simmer for 15 minutes or until macaroni is tender. **Yield:** 8 servings (2 quarts). **Diabetic Exchanges:** One 1-cup serving (prepared with low-sodium broth and without added salt) equals 1 starch, 1 meat; also, 140 calories, 109 mg sodium, 18 mg cholesterol, 13 gm carbohydrate, 10 gm protein, 6 gm fat.

Zesty Corn Chowder
Jan Ecklor, Souderton, Pennsylvania

This chowder needs no simmering—it goes from stovetop to table in just minutes. So it's perfect when time is short and your family is hungry.

1-1/2 cups milk
    1 can (10-3/4 ounces) condensed cream of
        potato soup, undiluted
    1 can (10-3/4 ounces) condensed cream of
        chicken soup, undiluted
    1 cup chicken broth
    2 cups cubed cooked chicken
    1 can (11 ounces) Mexican-style corn, undrained
    1 can (4 ounces) chopped green chilies
    1/2 cup sliced fresh mushrooms
1-1/2 cups (6 ounces) shredded cheddar cheese

In a 3-qt. saucepan, combine milk, soups and broth; blend well. Add all remaining ingredients except cheese. Heat through, stirring occasionally. Remove from the heat. Stir in cheese until melted. **Yield:** 6-8 servings (2 quarts).

Waldorf Sandwiches
Darlene Sutton, Arvada, Colorado
(PICTURED AT LEFT)

The fresh fruity filling for this sandwich is a nice variation of a classic. My clan loves the cool and creamy combination, so I serve these sandwiches often for a light lunch or dinner.

    1 can (20 ounces) crushed pineapple
    3 cups cubed cooked chicken
    1 medium red apple, chopped
    1 medium green apple, chopped
    1 cup chopped walnuts
    1 cup sliced celery
    1 cup mayonnaise
    1 tablespoon poppy seeds
    1 teaspoon sugar
    1 teaspoon grated lemon peel
  1/2 teaspoon vanilla extract
  1/2 teaspoon salt
Rolls, croissants *or* pita bread

Drain pineapple, pressing out excess juice; discard all but 1/4 cup juice. In a large bowl, combine pineapple, chicken, apples, walnuts and celery. In a small bowl, combine mayonnaise, poppy seeds, sugar, lemon peel, vanilla, salt and reserved pineapple juice. Pour over chicken mixture and toss well. Chill. Serve on rolls or croissants or in pita bread. **Yield:** 16 servings.

Bean, Chicken and Sausage Soup
Linda Johnson, Sevierville, Tennessee
(PICTURED AT LEFT)

I found this recipe in a magazine and have tried different ingredients through the years. My husband thinks this is the best version yet. I hope you enjoy it, too!

1-1/2 pounds bulk Italian sausage
    2 cups chopped onion
    6 bacon strips, diced
    2 quarts water
    2 cans (14-1/2 ounces *each*) tomatoes with liquid, cut up
    2 bay leaves
    2 teaspoons garlic powder
    1 teaspoon *each* dried thyme, savory and salt
  1/2 teaspoon *each* dried basil, oregano and pepper
    4 cups cubed cooked chicken
    2 cans (15 to 16 ounces *each*) great northern beans, rinsed and drained

In a heavy 8-qt. Dutch oven or soup kettle, cook sausage, onion and bacon over medium-high heat until sausage is no longer pink; drain. Add water, tomatoes and seasonings. Cover and simmer for 30 minutes. Add chicken and beans. Simmer, uncovered, for 30-45 minutes. Remove bay leaves before serving. **Yield:** 18 servings (4-1/2 quarts).

> **A LUSCIOUS LUNCH.** *Pictured at left: Waldorf Sandwiches and Bean, Chicken and Sausage Soup (both recipes on this page).*

California Clubs
Diane Cigel, Stevens Point, Wisconsin

When visiting our son in California, I sampled a delicious club sandwich. I came up with this recipe to capture the same flavor. One taste reminds me of that wonderful vacation.

  1/2 cup ranch salad dressing
  1/4 cup Dijon mustard
    8 slices sourdough bread
    4 boneless skinless chicken breast halves, cooked and sliced
    1 large tomato, sliced
    1 avocado, peeled and sliced
   12 bacon strips, cooked and drained

In a small bowl, combine salad dressing and mustard; spread on each slice of bread. On four slices of bread, layer chicken, tomato, avocado and bacon. Top with remaining bread. **Yield:** 4 servings.

Herbed Chicken Soup
Myrna Huebert, Tofield, Alberta

I love cooking from scratch and turning a recipe into my own personal "creation". This soup is one I developed gradually over the years…after some experimenting.

✓ This tasty dish uses less sugar, salt and fat. Recipe includes *Diabetic Exchanges*.

    1 broiler-fryer chicken (3 to 3-1/2 pounds), cut up
2-1/2 quarts water
    4 medium carrots, cut into 1/2-inch pieces
    1 medium onion, chopped
  1/2 cup chopped celery
    5 chicken bouillon cubes
    2 tablespoons dried parsley flakes
    1 tablespoon dried thyme
    1 teaspoon *each* dried sage and poultry seasoning
    1 teaspoon salt, optional
  1/2 teaspoon pepper
    1 large bay leaf
    1 package (12 ounces) frozen noodles *or* 2 cups cooked noodles

In a 4-qt. soup kettle, place all ingredients except noodles. Cover and bring to a boil; skim fat. Reduce heat; cover and and simmer for 1-1/2 hours or until chicken is tender. Remove chicken; allow to cool. Debone and cut into chunks. Skim fat from broth; bring to a boil. Return chicken to kettle. Add frozen noodles and cook for 20 minutes or until tender, or add cooked noodles and heat through. Remove bay leaf. **Yield:** 16 servings (4 quarts). **Diabetic Exchanges:** One 1-cup serving (prepared with low-sodium bouillon and without added salt) equals 1 lean meat, 1/2 starch; also, 91 calories, 181 mg sodium, 31 mg cholesterol, 8 gm carbohydrate, 11 gm protein, 2 gm fat.

Swedish Potato Dumpling Soup
Margaret Peterson, Genoa, Nebraska

Family and friends gather around our table throughout the year to enjoy good company and great food. As part of our traditional Christmas Eve meal, I serve this hearty soup.

✓ This tasty dish uses less sugar, salt and fat. Recipe includes *Diabetic Exchanges*.

   1 broiler-fryer chicken (3-1/2 to 4 pounds), cut up
6-1/2 cups water
   2 teaspoons salt, optional
   2 celery ribs, quartered
   1 medium carrot, quartered
   1 small onion, peeled
   4 whole peppercorns
   2 whole cloves
   2 whole allspice
   2 chicken bouillon cubes
   1 package (10 ounces) frozen green beans
   1 package (12 ounces) frozen noodles
DUMPLINGS:
   2 medium potatoes, cooked and mashed (without added milk or butter)
   1 egg, beaten *or* egg substitute equivalent
   2 tablespoons half-and-half cream
   1 teaspoon sugar
1/4 teaspoon salt, optional
1/2 cup all-purpose flour

In a 5-qt. soup kettle, combine the first 10 ingredients. Cover and bring to a boil. Reduce heat; simmer for 3 hours. Remove chicken; allow to cool. Strain broth, discarding vegetables and seasonings. Add enough water to make 8 cups; return to kettle. Debone chicken and cut into chunks; add to kettle with beans and noodles. Bring to a boil; cook for 20 minutes. For dumplings, mix potatoes, egg, cream, sugar and salt if desired in a medium bowl. Gradually add flour to make a stiff batter (it should form a peak when spoon is lifted). Drop by teaspoons into boiling soup. Cover and simmer for 3 minutes. **Yield:** 12 servings (3 quarts). **Diabetic Exchanges:** One 1-cup serving (prepared with egg substitute and low-sodium bouillon and without added salt) equals 2 lean meat, 1 starch; also, 192 calories, 62 mg sodium, 52 mg cholesterol, 15 gm carbohydrate, 19 gm protein, 6 gm fat.

Baked Chicken Sandwiches with Mushroom Sauce
Rebecca Magee, Chandler, Arizona

These baked sandwiches have been a tried-and-true brunch and luncheon dish at our house. No matter how many times I serve them, they always prompt recipe requests.

16 slices white sandwich bread
   8 slices Swiss cheese
   2 cups cubed cooked chicken
   4 eggs
2-1/2 cups milk
1/4 teaspoon pepper
   1 cup cornflake crumbs

   1 tablespoon butter *or* margarine, melted
MUSHROOM SAUCE:
   1 can (8 ounces) mushroom stems and pieces, drained
   2 tablespoons butter *or* margarine
   1 can (10-3/4 ounces) condensed cream of chicken soup, undiluted
1/2 cup milk
1/2 teaspoon dried thyme

In a greased 15-in. x 10-in. x 1-in. baking pan, arrange eight slices of bread. Place a slice of cheese on each; top with chicken and another slice of bread. Beat eggs, milk and pepper; pour over the sandwiches. Combine crumbs and butter; sprinkle over sandwiches. Bake at 350° for 1 hour and 20 minutes or until golden brown. Meanwhile, for sauce, saute mushrooms in butter. Add remaining ingredients; mix well. Heat through but do not boil. Spoon over sandwiches. **Yield:** 8 servings.

Matzo Ball Soup
Bernice Polak, New Smyrna Beach, Florida

My mother is of Russian descent and would make this for Friday night dinner while I was growing up. It's a very comforting soup that brings back many happy memories.

   1 broiler-fryer chicken (3-1/2 to 4 pounds), cut up
   2 quarts water
   6 carrots, cut in half lengthwise, then into 2-inch pieces
   1 large onion, peeled
   2 celery ribs, cut in half
   2 sprigs fresh dill (3 inches)
   1 can (49 ounces) chicken broth
   2 teaspoons salt
1/2 teaspoon pepper
   2 cups cooked noodles
MATZO BALLS:
   2 eggs
   1 cup matzo meal
   2 tablespoons chicken fat *or* shortening
   2 tablespoons minced fresh parsley
   2 teaspoons salt
Dash pepper
1/2 to 1 cup cold water

Place chicken and water in an 8-qt. soup kettle. Cover and bring to a boil; skim fat. Add carrots, onion and celery. Fold dill in half and wrap many times with thread or dental floss; add to soup. Bring to a boil. Reduce heat to medium-low; cover but keep lid ajar and simmer for 2-1/2 hours. Meanwhile, combine first six matzo ball ingredients in a medium bowl. Add enough water to make a thick pancake-like batter. Refrigerate for 2 hours (mixture thickens as it stands). Remove and discard onion, celery and dill from broth. Remove chicken and allow to cool; debone and cut into chunks. Skim fat from broth. Return chicken to kettle. Add canned broth, salt and pepper; bring to a boil. Reduce heat; cover and simmer. To complete matzo balls, bring 4 qts. water to a boil in a 5-qt. Dutch oven. With very wet hands, form heaping teaspoonfuls of batter into balls. If mixture is too thin, stir in 1-2 tablespoons of matzo meal. Drop balls into boiling water. (They will sink when dropped but will rise in a few minutes.) Cook for 10 minutes. Remove with slotted spoon and add to simmering soup. Add noodles; heat through. **Yield:** 18 servings (4-1/2 quarts).

Fried Chicken Pitas
Jennifer Veneziano, Carmel, Indiana

These pitas are very different from your usual chicken sandwiches—they use leftover fried chicken! No one will be able to resist these tasty treats.

- 3 cups thinly sliced fried chicken (including crispy skin)
- 1 cup bottled coleslaw dressing
- 1/3 cup crumbled cooked bacon
- 2 tablespoons chopped green onions with tops
- 1/4 teaspoon dry mustard
- 1/8 teaspoon pepper
- 6 pita bread halves

In a medium bowl, combine chicken, dressing, bacon, onions, mustard and pepper; mix well. Spoon into pita bread. **Yield:** 6 servings.

Chickenwiches
Janis Plourde, Smooth Rock Falls, Ontario

This is one of the best recipes I've found for using leftover chicken. The sandwiches are easy to prepare and make a nice brown-bag treat for our teenagers' lunches.

- 1 cup finely chopped cooked chicken
- 1/2 cup chopped celery
- 1/4 cup mayonnaise
- 2 tablespoons sliced stuffed green olives
- 2 tablespoons minced fresh parsley
- 2 teaspoons lemon juice
- 1/4 teaspoon salt

Dash pepper
- 6 slices sandwich bread
- 6 bacon strips, cooked and crumbled

In a medium bowl, combine the first eight ingredients; mix well. Spread on three slices of bread; sprinkle with bacon. Top with remaining bread. **Yield:** 3 servings.

Granny's Spicy Soup
Rose Rose, Akron, Ohio

My mother makes the best soups around and has become known to others as "The Soup Lady". When my kids ask me to make Granny's soup, I'm happy to oblige.

✓ This tasty dish uses less sugar, salt and fat. Recipe includes *Diabetic Exchanges*.

- 1 broiler-fryer chicken (3-1/2 to 4 pounds), cut up
- 2 quarts water
- 4 to 5 celery ribs with leaves, diced
- 2 medium carrots, diced
- 1 large onion, diced
- 1 to 1-1/2 teaspoons pickling spices
- 1-1/2 teaspoons salt, optional
- 4 chicken bouillon cubes
- 1/4 teaspoon pepper
- 1 cup uncooked noodles

Place chicken and water in a large soup kettle. Cover and bring to a boil; skim fat. Reduce heat; cover and simmer for 2 hours or until chicken falls off bone. Strain broth; return to kettle. Allow chicken to cool; debone and cut into chunks. Skim fat from broth. Return chicken to broth along with celery, carrots and onion. Place pickling spices in a tea ball or cheesecloth bag; add to soup. Bring to a boil. Reduce heat; cover and simmer for 1 hour. Remove spices; add salt if desired, bouillon, pepper and noodles. Cook for 10-15 minutes or until noodles are tender. **Yield:** 12 servings (about 3 quarts). **Editor's Note:** The soup gets its name from the pickling spices, not from being hot. **Diabetic Exchanges:** One 1-cup serving (prepared with low-sodium bouillon and without added salt) equals 1 lean meat, 1 vegetable, 1/2 starch; also, 114 calories, 74 mg sodium, 32 mg cholesterol, 9 gm carbohydrate, 14 gm protein, 3 gm fat.

Make-Ahead Saucy Sandwiches
Elizabeth Rothert, Kernville, California

I've made these sandwiches many times for luncheons and light dinners. They can be prepared ahead of time and popped in the oven when needed.

- 24 slices white sandwich bread
- 1-1/2 cups diced cooked chicken
- 1 can (10-3/4 ounces) condensed cream of mushroom soup, undiluted
- 1/2 cup prepared chicken gravy
- 1 can (8 ounces) water chestnuts, drained and chopped
- 1 jar (2 ounces) chopped pimientos, drained
- 2 tablespoons chopped green onions

Salt and pepper to taste
- 5 eggs
- 1/3 cup milk
- 2 bags (6 ounces *each*) ridged potato chips, crushed

Trim crusts from bread; discard or save for another use. In a medium bowl, combine chicken, soup, gravy, water chestnuts, pimientos, onions, salt and pepper. Spread on 12 slices of bread; top with remaining bread. Wrap each in foil and freeze. In a bowl, beat eggs and milk. Unwrap sandwiches; dip frozen sandwiches in egg mixture and then in potato chips. Place on greased baking sheets. Bake at 300° for 1 hour or until golden brown. **Yield:** 12 servings. **Editor's Note:** Unbaked sandwiches may be frozen for up to 2 months.

> **BETTER BROTH.** For a superbly seasoned chicken stock, try this: Add 1 large chopped onion, 1 to 2 cups celery leaves, 2 chicken bouillon cubes, 1 chopped carrot and 1 teaspoon salt to chicken parts and water. Simmer for 1 hour; strain and use for soup.

Wild Rice Soup

Tracey Zeman, Zimmerman, Minnesota
(PICTURED AT LEFT)

Spending time in the kitchen has never been my hobby. When I got married and started a family, it became a necessity. This simple but satisfying soup makes me look like a fabulous cook!

      3 cans (10-1/2 ounces *each*) condensed chicken broth
      2 cups water
  1/2 cup uncooked wild rice
  1/2 cup sliced green onions
  1/2 cup butter *or* margarine
  3/4 cup all-purpose flour
  3/4 teaspoon salt
  1/2 teaspoon poultry seasoning
  1/4 teaspoon pepper
      2 cups light cream
      2 cups cubed cooked chicken
      1 jar (2 ounces) chopped pimientos, drained

In a large saucepan, combine the broth, water and rice; bring to a boil. Reduce heat; cover and simmer for 35-40 minutes or until rice is tender. In a medium saucepan, saute onions in butter over low heat. Stir in flour, salt, poultry seasoning and pepper. Cook, stirring constantly, until bubbly and thickened. Stir in cream; cook for 6 minutes or until mixture thickens slightly, stirring constantly. Stir into rice mixture. Add chicken and pimientos; heat through. **Yield:** 6-8 servings (about 2 quarts).

Tex-Mex Chicken Soup

MayDell Spiess, Industry, Texas
(PICTURED AT LEFT)

We keep busy here on our ranch. So I'm always looking for dishes that can be prepared in a hurry but are still filling and tasty. This quick and easy soup is a real winner!

✓ This tasty dish uses less sugar, salt and fat. Recipe includes *Diabetic Exchanges*.

  1/2 cup chopped onion
      2 garlic cloves, minced
      1 tablespoon cooking oil
      4 cups chicken broth
      3 cups cubed cooked chicken
      3 medium zucchini, sliced
      1 can (14-1/2 ounces) tomatoes with liquid, cut up
      1 can (11 ounces) whole kernel corn, drained
      1 can (8 ounces) tomato sauce
  1/2 cup salsa
      2 teaspoons ground cumin
      1 teaspoon salt, optional
  3/4 teaspoon pepper

  1/2 teaspoon dried oregano
Shredded cheddar cheese, optional
Tortilla chips, optional

In a 4-qt. soup kettle, saute onion and garlic in oil until tender. Add the next 11 ingredients; bring to a boil. Reduce heat; cover and simmer for 30 minutes. If desired, top individual servings with cheese and serve with tortilla chips. **Yield:** 12 servings (3 quarts). **Diabetic Exchanges:** One 1-cup serving (prepared with low-sodium broth, tomatoes, corn and tomato sauce and without added salt, cheese and tortilla chips) equals 1 vegetable, 1/2 starch, 1/2 fat; also, 91 calories, 109 mg sodium, 21 mg cholesterol, 10 gm carbohydrate, 8 gm protein, 3 gm fat.

Grandma's Chicken 'n' Dumpling Soup

Paulette Balda, Prophetstown, Illinois
(PICTURED AT LEFT)

I've enjoyed making this rich soup for some 30 years. Every time I serve it, I remember my grandma, who was very special to me and was known as a great cook.

      1 broiler-fryer chicken (3-1/2 to 4 pounds), cut up
  2-1/4 quarts cold water
      5 chicken bouillon cubes
      6 whole peppercorns
      3 whole cloves
      1 can (10-3/4 ounces) condensed cream of chicken soup, undiluted
      1 can (10-3/4 ounces) condensed cream of mushroom soup, undiluted
  1-1/2 cups chopped carrots
      1 cup fresh *or* frozen peas
      1 cup chopped celery
      1 cup chopped peeled potatoes
  1/4 cup chopped onion
  1-1/2 teaspoons seasoned salt
  1/4 teaspoon pepper
      1 bay leaf
DUMPLINGS:
      2 cups all-purpose flour
      4 teaspoons baking powder
      1 teaspoon salt
  1/4 teaspoon pepper
      1 egg, beaten
      2 tablespoons butter *or* margarine, melted
  3/4 to 1 cup milk
Snipped fresh parsley, optional

Place chicken, water, bouillon, peppercorns and cloves in an 8-qt. Dutch oven or soup kettle. Cover and bring to a boil; skim fat. Reduce heat; cover and simmer 1-1/2 hours or until chicken is tender. Strain broth; return to kettle. Allow chicken to cool; debone and cut into chunks. Skim fat from broth. Return chicken to kettle with soups, vegetables and seasonings; bring to a boil. Reduce heat; cover and simmer for 1 hour. Uncover; increase heat to a gentle boil. Remove bay leaf. For dumplings, combine dry ingredients in a medium bowl. Stir in egg, butter and enough milk to make a moist stiff batter. Drop by teaspoonfuls into soup. Cover and cook without lifting the lid for 18-20 minutes. Sprinkle with parsley if desired. **Yield:** 12 servings (3 quarts).

SOUPER ASSORTMENT. *Pictured at left, top to bottom: Wild Rice Soup, Tex-Mex Chicken Soup and Grandma's Chicken 'n' Dumpling Soup (recipes on this page).*

Country-Fried Favorites

The oven-baked and pan-fried chicken classics found here are bound to become frequently requested standbys in many country kitchens...including yours!

Mustard Drumsticks for Two
Virginia LeJeune, Agassiz, British Columbia
(PICTURED AT LEFT)

I come from a large family and learned to cook when I was very young. This perfectly portioned dish comes in handy now that I'm cooking for just the two of us.

> 2 tablespoons *each* mayonnaise, vegetable oil and prepared mustard
> 1/2 cup crushed butter-flavored crackers
> 1 teaspoon chili powder
> 4 chicken legs, skin removed

In a small bowl, combine mayonnaise, oil and mustard. In a plastic bag, combine crackers and chili powder. Dip chicken legs in mustard mixture, then shake in crumbs. Place in a greased 8-in. square baking dish. Bake, uncovered, at 400° for 35-40 minutes or until juices run clear. **Yield:** 2 servings.

Creamy Pan-Fried Chicken
Naden Hewko, Cactus Lake, Saskatchewan
(PICTURED AT LEFT)

In this recipe, a rich creamy mushroom sauce pairs nicely with crunchy, tender chicken. It's a one-of-a-kind meal that will have your family asking for seconds!

> 1 egg
> 1 tablespoon milk
> 3/4 cup plus 2 tablespoons all-purpose flour, *divided*
> 1-1/2 teaspoons salt, *divided*
> 1/2 teaspoon curry powder
> 1/4 teaspoon pepper
> 1 broiler-fryer chicken (3 to 3-1/2 pounds), cut up
> 1/4 cup cooking oil
> 4 green onions, sliced
> 1 cup sliced fresh mushrooms
> 2 tablespoons minced fresh dill *or* 2 teaspoons dill weed
> 2 cups half-and-half cream

In a medium bowl, beat egg and milk. In another bowl, combine 3/4 cup flour, 1 teaspoon salt, curry powder and pepper. Dip chicken pieces in egg mixture, then in flour mixture. Heat oil in a large skillet; brown chicken pieces on both sides. Cover and cook over low heat for 45 minutes or until juices run clear. Remove chicken from skillet and keep warm. Discard all but 1 tablespoon drippings;

DOWN-HOME DINNER. *Pictured at left, top to bottom: Mustard Drumsticks for Two and Creamy Pan-Fried Chicken (both recipes on this page).*

saute onions and mushrooms in drippings over medium heat until tender. Stir in dill and remaining salt. In a bowl, combine a small amount of cream with remaining flour; mix until smooth. Add to skillet along with remaining cream; bring to a boil, stirring constantly. Cook and stir for 1-2 minutes. Serve with the chicken. **Yield:** 4 servings.

Picnic Potato Chip Chicken
Kim Joseph, Jacksonville, North Carolina

This crunchy chicken could always be found in the picnic basket Mom took to potlucks. For a little variety, try coating with barbecue-flavored potato chips.

> 3 cups crushed ridged potato chips (any flavor)
> 3/4 to 1 teaspoon garlic powder
> 1 broiler-fryer chicken (3-1/2 to 4 pounds), cut up
> 1/2 cup butter *or* margarine, melted

In a shallow bowl, combine potato chips and garlic powder. Dip chicken pieces in butter, then roll in potato chip mixture. Place in a greased 15-in. x 10-in. x 1-in. baking pan. Sprinkle with any remaining butter and coating. Bake, uncovered, at 350° for 1 hour or until juices run clear. **Yield:** 4 servings.

Southern-Fried Fryer
Jan Watrin, Sandstone, Minnesota

When my family has a hankering for down-home Southern cooking, they ask me to serve this hearty chicken. They savor the traditional fried flavor.

> 1 broiler-fryer chicken (3-1/2 to 4 pounds), cut up
> 1 egg
> 1 cup vegetable oil
> 1 to 2 garlic cloves, minced
> 1/2 teaspoon dried rosemary, crushed
> 1/2 teaspoon *each* paprika, dried oregano and tarragon
> 1-1/2 cups all-purpose flour
> 2 teaspoons salt, *divided*
> 3/4 teaspoon pepper
> 2 cups cooking oil

Place chicken in a 13-in. x 9-in. x 2-in. glass baking dish. In a small bowl, beat egg; add oil, garlic and seasonings. Pour over chicken, turning pieces to coat well. Cover and refrigerate for 2 hours. Combine flour, 1-1/2 teaspoons salt and pepper. Drain chicken, discarding marinade. Dredge chicken in flour mixture. Heat oil in a 12-in. skillet or Dutch oven over medium-high heat. Brown chicken on all sides. Sprinkle with remaining salt. Cover; reduce heat to medium-low and cook for 30-40 minutes or until juices run clear. **Yield:** 4 servings.

Baked Crumbled Chicken
Dorothy Schmidt, Falun, Alberta

I can quickly prepare this chicken, bake it and have a hearty meal waiting for my husband at the end of the day. It's just right for his unpredictable farmer's schedule!

- 1-1/2 cups crushed cornflakes
- 2 tablespoons minced fresh parsley
- 2 teaspoons paprika
- 1-1/2 teaspoons salt
- 1-1/2 teaspoons dried basil
- 1/2 teaspoon pepper
- 2 eggs
- 1/2 cup milk
- 1 broiler-fryer chicken (3-1/2 to 4 pounds), cut up
- 1/4 cup butter *or* margarine, melted

In a shallow bowl or large resealable plastic bag, combine cornflakes, parsley, paprika, salt, basil and pepper. In another bowl, beat eggs and milk. Dip chicken pieces in egg mixture, then coat generously with crumb mixture. Place in an ungreased 13-in. x 9-in. x 2-in. baking dish. Drizzle with butter. Bake, uncovered, at 375° for 50-60 minutes or until golden brown and juices run clear. **Yield:** 4 servings.

Sweet 'n' Nutty Fried Chicken
Cecelia Wilson, Rockville, Connecticut

I came up with this recipe when I wanted to try something a little different. Everyone liked the golden crunchy coating.

- 2 cups Special K cereal
- 1 cup sugar-and-honey-flavored wheat germ
- 2 tablespoons dry onion soup mix
- 1/4 teaspoon pepper
- 1 broiler-fryer chicken (3-1/2 to 4 pounds), cut up
- 1/2 cup butter *or* margarine, melted

In a food processor or blender, combine cereal, wheat germ, onion soup mix and pepper; process until mixture resembles fine crumbs. Dip chicken in butter, then coat generously with cereal mixture. Place in a greased 13-in. x 9-in. x 2-in. baking dish. Bake, uncovered, at 350° for 1 hour or until juices run clear. **Yield:** 4 servings.

Savory Seasoned Chicken
Linda Dyck, Austin, Manitoba

My mother-in-law shared this treasured recipe with me. It's long been a family favorite and is always welcome whenever I offer it to family and friends.

- 1-1/2 cups all-purpose flour
- 1 tablespoon salt
- 2 teaspoons pepper
- 1-1/2 teaspoons meat tenderizer, optional
- 1/4 teaspoon *each* curry powder, garlic powder, onion powder, dry mustard and ground sage

- 1/8 teaspoon ground turmeric
- 1/8 teaspoon ground cloves
- 1 egg
- 1/2 cup milk
- 1 broiler-fryer chicken (3-1/2 to 4 pounds), cut up

Cooking oil for deep-fat frying

In a shallow bowl or large resealable plastic bag, combine dry ingredients. In another bowl, beat egg and milk. Dip chicken in egg mixture, then dredge or shake in flour mixture. In a deep-fat fryer, heat oil to 365°. Fry chicken, several pieces at a time, for 5 minutes or until golden brown, turning once. Place in an ungreased 13-in. x 9-in. x 2-in. baking dish. Bake, uncovered, at 400° for 20 minutes or until juices run clear. **Yield:** 4 servings.

Tortilla Chicken with Cheese Sauce
Regena Thompson, Emporia, Kansas

Our children are grown and out of the nest, but when they come home, they frequently request this for dinner. The creamy cheese sauce complements the spicy chicken.

- 1/2 cup all-purpose flour
- 1 envelope taco seasoning mix
- 1/2 teaspoon salt
- 8 chicken thighs, skin removed
- 1/4 cup butter *or* margarine, melted
- 1-3/4 cups crushed tortilla chips (about 9 ounces)

CHEESE SAUCE:
- 2 tablespoons finely chopped onion
- 2 tablespoons butter *or* margarine
- 2 tablespoons plus 1 teaspoon all-purpose flour
- 1 can (12 ounces) evaporated milk
- 1 cup cubed Monterey Jack cheese
- 1 can (2-1/4 ounces) sliced ripe olives, drained
- 1 teaspoon lemon juice
- 1/2 teaspoon salt
- 1/4 teaspoon hot pepper sauce
- 1/8 teaspoon pepper

In a shallow bowl or large resealable plastic bag, combine flour, taco seasoning and salt. Dredge chicken. Dip chicken in butter, then coat with tortillas. Place in an ungreased 11-in. x 7-in. x 2-in. baking dish. Bake, uncovered, at 350° for 50-60 minutes or until juices run clear. Meanwhile, for cheese sauce, saute onion in butter in a medium saucepan until softened. Stir in flour and cook until bubbly. Slowly whisk in milk; cook over medium-low heat until thickened and bubbly. Stir in remaining sauce ingredients. Cook and stir until cheese melts. Serve with chicken. **Yield:** 4 servings.

THE THICKER, THE BETTER. For extra-crispy fried chicken, dip the chicken pieces in buttermilk and then coat with all-purpose flour. The buttermilk holds more flour on the chicken for a thicker coating.

Ginger Batter Chicken
Teresa Scholz, Marion, Ohio

The puffy golden batter and hint of spices in this recipe makes the moist chicken irresistible. Folks who sample this can't believe it's so simple to prepare.

- 1 broiler-fryer chicken (3-1/2 to 4 pounds), cut up
- 2 teaspoons salt
- 2 teaspoons dried rosemary, crushed
- 1/2 cup water
- Cooking oil for deep-fat frying
- GINGER BATTER:
- 1-1/4 cups all-purpose flour
- 1 teaspoon baking powder
- 1 teaspoon salt
- 1/2 teaspoon ground ginger
- 1 egg
- 1 cup milk
- 1/4 cup vegetable oil

Place chicken pieces in an ungreased 13-in. x 9-in. x 2-in. baking dish. Sprinkle with salt and rosemary; add water. Cover and bake at 350° for 1 hour. Remove chicken to paper towels. Cool 10 minutes; remove skin and pat dry. In a deep-fat fryer, heat oil to 350°. For batter, combine flour, baking powder, salt and ginger. Add egg, milk and oil; beat until smooth. Dip chicken, one piece at a time, in batter. Fry chicken in hot oil for 3-5 minutes or until golden brown. Drain on paper towels and keep warm. **Yield:** 4-6 servings. **Editor's Note:** Chicken will be more tender if skin is removed after baking.

Marinated Baked Chicken Breasts
Donna Coble, Burlington, North Carolina

To better control my food allergies, I do a lot of cooking from scratch. Good thing it's one of my favorite pastimes! This is a popular Sunday lunch at our house.

- 1 cup (8 ounces) sour cream
- 2 tablespoons lemon juice
- 2 teaspoons Worcestershire sauce
- 2 teaspoons celery salt, *divided*
- 2 teaspoons paprika, *divided*
- 1-1/2 teaspoons salt
- 1 teaspoon pepper, *divided*
- 3/4 teaspoon garlic powder, *divided*
- 6 chicken breast halves
- 3/4 cup crushed butter-flavored crackers
- 1/2 cup butter *or* margarine, melted, *divided*

In a large shallow bowl, combine sour cream, lemon juice, Worcestershire sauce, half of the celery salt and paprika, salt, and half of the pepper and garlic powder. Add chicken; turn to coat well. Cover and refrigerate at least 4 hours. Meanwhile, in a large bag or another bowl, combine crackers and remaining seasonings. Drain chicken, discarding marinade. Shake or dredge chicken in crumb mixture. Place in an ungreased jelly roll or broiler pan; drizzle with 1/4 cup butter. Bake, uncovered, at 325° for 45 minutes. Drizzle with remaining butter; bake 45 minutes longer or until juices run clear. **Yield:** 4-6 servings.

Golden Chicken
Alberta Garver, Hereford, Colorado

(PICTURED ON FRONT COVER)

The mildly seasoned coating makes this chicken tender and juicy. I'm sure your family will enjoy the old-fashioned flavor and appearance as much as mine does.

- 2 cups all-purpose flour
- 2 cups crushed stone-ground wheat crackers (about 50 crackers)
- 2 tablespoons salt
- 2 tablespoons paprika
- 2 tablespoons vegetable oil
- 1 tablespoon sugar
- 1-1/4 teaspoons pepper
- 1 teaspoon garlic powder
- 1 broiler-fryer chicken (3-1/2 to 4 pounds), cut up
- 1 cup club soda *or* milk

Combine first eight ingredients in a large bowl; mix well. Place 1-1/2 cups in a resealable plastic bag. Store remaining coating in a covered container in the refrigerator for future use. Dip chicken in soda or milk, then place in bag; seal and shake to coat. Place chicken in a single layer in a greased 13-in. x 9-in. x 2-in. baking pan. Bake, uncovered, at 375° for 50-60 minutes or until juices run clear. **Yield:** 4 servings (4-1/2 cups coating).

Herb Chicken with Mustard Sauce
Sue Broyles, Cherokee, Texas

A wonderful blend of herbs gives this chicken its appealing flavor. And the mustard sauce adds a little "zip". I know you'll agree baked chicken never tasted so good!

- 1/2 cup crushed cornflakes
- 1/4 cup yellow cornmeal
- 2 teaspoons dried basil
- 2 teaspoons salt
- 1 teaspoon dried tarragon
- 1/2 teaspoon pepper
- 4 boneless skinless chicken breast halves
- 1/2 cup buttermilk
- MUSTARD SAUCE:
- 1 cup chicken broth
- 2 teaspoons cornstarch
- 1/4 cup Dijon mustard
- 1/4 cup sour cream

In a shallow bowl or large resealable plastic bag, combine the first six ingredients. Dip chicken in buttermilk, then coat with crumb mixture. Place in a single layer in a greased 13-in. x 9-in. x 2-in. baking dish. Sprinkle with remaining crumbs. Bake, uncovered, at 375° for 25-30 minutes or until juices run clear. Meanwhile, for the sauce, bring broth and cornstarch to a boil in a small saucepan. Stir in mustard; simmer for 3 minutes. Add sour cream; heat through, stirring constantly (do not boil). Serve over chicken. **Yield:** 4 servings.

Oatmeal Baked Chicken
Ena Quiggle, Goodhue, Minnesota
(PICTURED AT LEFT)

This recipe proves you can have fried chicken without a lot of fuss. The chili powder and cumin add a subtle spiciness that appeals to everyone.

✓ **This tasty dish uses less sugar, salt and fat. Recipe includes** *Diabetic Exchanges*.

1-1/2 cups quick-cooking oats
1 tablespoon paprika
1 tablespoon chili powder
1 teaspoon salt, optional
3/4 teaspoon garlic powder
1/2 teaspoon ground cumin
1/4 teaspoon pepper
1 broiler-fryer chicken (3-1/2 to 4 pounds), cut up
1/2 cup milk
2 tablespoons butter *or* margarine, melted

Coat a 13-in. x 9-in. x 2-in. baking dish with nonstick cooking spray; set aside. In a shallow bowl or large resealable plastic bag, combine oats, paprika, chili powder, salt if desired, garlic powder, cumin and pepper. Dip chicken in milk, then coat with oat mixture. Place in prepared baking dish. Drizzle with butter. Bake, uncovered, at 375° for 45-50 minutes or until juices run clear. **Yield:** 4 servings. **Diabetic Exchanges:** One serving (prepared with skim milk and margarine and without added salt) equals 3 lean meat, 1-1/2 starch, 1 fat; also, 316 calories, 146 mg sodium, 62 mg cholesterol, 24 gm carbohydrate, 28 gm protein, 12 gm fat.

Coconut Chicken with Pineapple Vinaigrette
Myrtis Hagee, Hiwasse, Arkansas

It's easy to bring a tropical taste to your table with this interesting chicken dish. The vinaigrette adds a nice tart touch to the slightly sweet coconut coating.

1 cup crushed shredded wheat cereal
3/4 cup flaked coconut
1 broiler-fryer chicken (3-1/2 to 4 pounds), cut up
2 eggs, beaten
1/3 cup water
1/3 cup vinegar
1 tablespoon *each* cornstarch and sugar
1 tablespoon butter *or* margarine
1/2 cup chopped green pepper
1 small onion, chopped
1 cup drained pineapple chunks
1 tablespoon chopped pimientos

In a shallow bowl, combine cereal and coconut. Remove skin from chicken if desired. Dip chicken pieces in eggs, then coat with coconut mixture. Place in a greased 13-in. x 9-in. x 2-in. baking dish. Bake, uncovered, at 375° for

---

50-60 minutes or until juices run clear. Meanwhile, in a small saucepan, combine water, vinegar, cornstarch, sugar and butter. Cook over medium heat until thickened and bubbly, stirring constantly. Add green pepper and onion; cook until onion is softened. Stir in pineapple and pimientos; heat through. Serve with chicken. **Yield:** 4 servings.

Famous Fried Chicken
Helen Breyer, Antigo, Wisconsin

This fried chicken tastes even better cold the next day. But with such great flavor, there are never any leftovers…no matter how much I make!

3/4 cup all-purpose flour
3/4 cup buttermilk baking mix
3-1/2 teaspoons seasoned salt
1-1/2 teaspoons chili powder
1/2 teaspoon salt
1/4 teaspoon garlic powder
1 egg
1/2 cup milk
1 broiler-fryer chicken (3-1/2 to 4 pounds), cut up
Cooking oil for deep-fat frying

In a shallow bowl or large resealable plastic bag, combine dry ingredients. In a shallow bowl, beat egg and milk. Dip chicken pieces in egg mixture, then dredge or shake in flour mixture. In a deep-fat fryer, heat oil to 365°. Fry chicken, several pieces at a time, until browned on all sides, about 4 minutes. Place in an ungreased 13-in. x 9-in. x 2-in. baking dish. Bake, uncovered, at 350° for 40 minutes or until juices run clear. **Yield:** 4 servings.

Oven-Baked Sesame Chicken
Anne Smith, Taylors, South Carolina

Chicken is one of my family's favorite meats and I prepare it several different ways. This melt-in-your-mouth baked chicken is a much-requested entree for Sunday dinner.

4 boneless skinless chicken breast halves
1 cup buttermilk
1/3 cup butter *or* margarine, melted
1 tablespoon lemon juice
1 garlic clove, minced
1 cup dry bread crumbs
1/4 cup sesame seeds
1 tablespoon grated Parmesan cheese
1 teaspoon salt
1/4 teaspoon white pepper

Place chicken in a large resealable plastic bag; add buttermilk. Seal bag and refrigerate for at least 4 hours. In a shallow bowl, combine butter, lemon juice and garlic. In another bowl, combine bread crumbs, sesame seeds, Parmesan cheese, salt and pepper. Drain chicken, discarding buttermilk; dry on paper towels. Dip chicken in butter mixture, then coat with crumb mixture. Place in an ungreased 11-in. x 7-in. x 2-in. baking dish. Drizzle with remaining butter mixture. Bake, uncovered, at 450° for 10 minutes. Reduce heat to 350° and bake an additional 20 minutes or until juices run clear. **Yield:** 4 servings.

BOUNTIFUL BASKET. *Pictured at left: Oatmeal Baked Chicken (recipe on this page).*

Tasty Texas Tenders
Joan Dinger, Fulshear, Texas

When time gets away from you and your clan is hungry, prepare this fun fast finger food. The chicken is crispy outside and tender inside. Kids of all ages will love it!

- 1 pound chicken tenders *or* boneless skinless chicken breasts
- 3 cups crisp rice cereal, crushed
- 1 teaspoon garlic salt
- 1 teaspoon dill weed
- 1/4 cup vegetable oil
- Sour cream, optional

If using chicken breasts, cut into 4-in. strips; set aside. Combine cereal, garlic salt and dill. Dip chicken tenders or strips in oil, then roll in cereal mixture. Place on a foil-lined cookie sheet. Bake, uncovered, at 350° for 30 minutes or until juices run clear. Serve with sour cream for dipping if desired. **Yield:** 4-6 servings.

Onion-Baked Chicken
Barbara Erwin, Shipman, Illinois

Toasted onion is the deliciously different ingredient in the coating for this chicken. Folks will think you were in the kitchen all day making this quick and easy dish.

- 1/2 cup spicy brown mustard
- 1/4 cup soy sauce
- 2 tablespoons dried minced onion
- 1 cup dry bread crumbs *or* crushed cornflakes
- 1/2 teaspoon chicken bouillon granules
- 4 boneless skinless chicken breast halves

Combine mustard and soy sauce in a shallow bowl; set aside. In a small skillet, toast onion over medium heat until lightly browned, about 3 minutes. Pour into a shallow bowl. Add crumbs and bouillon; mix well. Dip chicken in mustard mixture, then coat with crumb mixture. Place on a rack over a greased baking sheet. Bake, uncovered, at 350° for 25 minutes or until juices run clear. **Yield:** 4 servings.

Sesame Fried Chicken
Helen Brown, Claypool, Indiana

I came up with this recipe one day as an alternative to traditional fried chicken. Everyone in my family raves about the sesame seed coating and special gravy.

- 1 cup all-purpose flour
- 3 tablespoons sesame seeds, toasted
- 1-1/2 teaspoons ground sage
- 1 teaspoon dried thyme
- 1/2 teaspoon paprika
- 6 boneless skinless chicken breast halves *or* 12 boneless skinless chicken thighs
- 1/2 cup milk
- Cooking oil

- 2 cups chicken broth
- Salt and pepper to taste

In a shallow bowl or large resealable plastic bag, combine flour, sesame seeds, sage, thyme and paprika. Reserve 1/4 cup and set aside. Dip chicken in milk, then dredge or shake in remaining flour mixture. Heat 1/2 in. of oil in a large skillet over medium heat. Fry chicken on both sides until golden brown and juices run clear, about 8 minutes. Remove chicken and keep warm. Drain oil, leaving drippings in pan. Stir in reserved flour mixture until bubbly; add chicken broth. Cook and stir until thickened and bubbly. Cook and stir 1 minute more. Season with salt and pepper. Serve with chicken. **Yield:** 6 servings. **Variation:** Cut chicken into strips before coating with flour mixture and use the gravy as a dipping sauce.

Ranch-Style Thighs
Marion Stanley, Joseph, Oregon

My family prefers oven-fried chicken to the deep-fried variety. Creamy ranch dressing makes this wonderfully crunchy chicken tender and juicy.

- 1/2 cup dry bread crumbs
- 1/4 cup grated Parmesan cheese
- 2 tablespoons yellow cornmeal
- 1/2 teaspoon Italian seasoning
- 6 chicken thighs (skin removed if desired)
- 1/2 cup ranch salad dressing

In a shallow bowl or large resealable plastic bag, combine crumbs, Parmesan cheese, cornmeal and Italian seasoning. Dip chicken in salad dressing, then coat with crumb mixture. Place in a greased 13-in. x 9-in. x 2-in. baking dish. Bake, uncovered, at 375° for 45-50 minutes or until juices run clear. **Yield:** 3-4 servings.

Pecan Oven-Fried Fryer
Mildred Troupe, Wartrace, Tennessee

This recipe combines two Southern classics—chicken and pecans. Although this chicken is baked in the oven, the rich nutty mixture gives it a fabulous fried flair.

- 1-1/2 cups buttermilk baking mix
- 3/4 cup finely chopped pecans
- 1 tablespoon paprika
- 1-1/2 teaspoons salt
- 3/4 teaspoon pepper
- 3/4 teaspoon poultry seasoning
- 1 broiler-fryer chicken (3-1/2 to 4 pounds), cut up
- 1 can (5 ounces) evaporated milk
- 1/2 cup butter *or* margarine, melted

In a shallow bowl or large resealable plastic bag, combine baking mix, pecans, paprika, salt, pepper and poultry seasoning. Dip chicken pieces in milk, then coat generously with pecan mixture. Place in a greased 13-in. x 9-in. x 2-in. baking dish. Drizzle with butter. Bake, uncovered, at 350° for 1 hour or until juices run clear. **Yield:** 4 servings.

Horse-Show Chicken

Mary Ann Morgan, Powder Springs, Georgia

When our children were young, we'd attend a local horse show every Saturday night. During our fun-filled evening, we would nibble on this tasty chicken.

    8 chicken breast quarters, skin removed
1/2 cup buttermilk
    2 cups all-purpose flour
    1 teaspoon salt
1/2 teaspoon *each* black pepper, white pepper,
       paprika, chili powder and poultry seasoning
Cooking oil for deep-fat frying

Place chicken in a 13-in. x 9-in. x 2-in. glass baking dish; pour buttermilk over. Cover and refrigerate 4 hours or overnight. Drain chicken, discarding buttermilk. In a shallow bowl or large resealable plastic bag, combine flour and seasonings; dredge chicken pieces. Place on waxed paper for 15 minutes to dry. In a deep-fat fryer, heat oil to 365°. Fry chicken, several pieces at a time, for about 10 minutes, turning once, or until chicken is dark brown and crispy and juices run clear. Drain on paper towels. **Yield:** 6-8 servings.

Creole Fried Chicken

Rachel Patton, Venice, Louisiana

The recipe for this creamy pan-fried chicken was given to me by my husband's grandmother. I make it at least twice a month—much to the delight of my family!

    1 cup all-purpose flour
    2 teaspoons salt
1-1/2 teaspoons creole seasoning
1/2 teaspoon pepper
    1 broiler-fryer chicken (3-1/2 to 4 pounds), cut up
    3 tablespoons cooking oil
    2 cups water

In a shallow bowl or large resealable plastic bag, combine dry ingredients. Dredge chicken. Heat oil in a large skillet; fry chicken, a few pieces at a time, until brown on all sides. Add water; bring to a boil. Reduce heat; cover and simmer for 45 minutes or until juices run clear. Thicken gravy if desired. **Yield:** 4 servings.

Chicken Parmesan

Sylvia Dirks, Clearbrook, British Columbia

With two small children, I appreciate meals that can be easily assembled and put into the oven. I always keep the ingredients for this festive chicken on hand.

3/4 cup grated Parmesan cheese
3/4 cup wheat germ, toasted
1-1/4 teaspoons salt
1/2 teaspoon *each* garlic powder, onion powder
       and dried oregano
1/2 teaspoon dried rosemary, crushed
1/4 teaspoon pepper

    1 broiler-fryer chicken (3-1/2 to 4 pounds), cut up
    1 cup buttermilk

In a shallow bowl or large resealable plastic bag, combine Parmesan cheese, wheat germ and seasonings. Dip chicken pieces in buttermilk, then coat with Parmesan mixture. Place in a greased 13-in. x 9-in. x 2-in. baking dish. Bake, uncovered, at 350° for 1 hour or until juices run clear. **Yield:** 4 servings.

Saucy Skillet Chicken

Myrtle Brandt, Morris, Manitoba

I created this extra-special skillet fried chicken for a graduation banquet. Days after the party, people were calling to get the recipe...I was happy to pass it on.

3/4 cup all-purpose flour
    2 teaspoons salt
1-1/2 teaspoons pepper
3/4 teaspoon meat tenderizer, optional
1/8 teaspoon *each* ground turmeric, curry powder,
       onion powder, garlic powder, dry mustard and
       dried sage
Pinch ground cloves
    6 boneless skinless chicken breast halves
1/4 cup butter *or* margarine
1-1/2 cups heavy cream
Hot mashed potatoes, optional

Combine flour and seasonings in a shallow bowl or large resealable plastic bag. Dredge or shake chicken in flour mixture. In a large skillet, cook chicken in butter over medium heat until browned on both sides. Pour cream over chicken; cover and simmer for 30 minutes. Serve sauce over chicken and mashed potatoes if desired. **Yield:** 4-6 servings.

Extra-Crispy Italian Chicken

Faye Wolf, Camden, Indiana

A cousin shared this recipe with me several years ago. Since then, I've made it too many times to count! I especially like to serve this chicken to guests because it's very attractive.

1-1/4 cups pancake mix
    2 envelopes (.6 ounce *each*) zesty Italian salad
       dressing mix
    1 egg
1/3 cup club soda
    1 broiler-fryer chicken (3-1/2 to 4 pounds), cut up
Cooking oil for deep-fat frying

In a shallow bowl or large resealable plastic bag, combine pancake mix and one envelope salad dressing mix. Combine the second envelope of salad dressing mix with the egg and club soda. Dip chicken pieces in egg mixture, then coat with the seasoned pancake mix. Place chicken pieces on a rack; allow to dry 5 minutes. In a deep-fat fryer, heat oil to 375°. Fry chicken, several pieces at a time, for 6 minutes or until golden brown. Place on an ungreased 15-in. x 10-in. x 1-in. baking pan. Bake, uncovered, at 350° for 30 minutes or until juices run clear. **Yield:** 4 servings.

Skillet Specialties

When you need dinner to go from stovetop to tabletop in a snap, reach for this assortment of scrumptious stir-frys, stews...and so much more!

Harvest Chicken
Linda Hutton, Hayden, Idaho
(PICTURED AT LEFT)

This chicken has become a Sunday-dinner standby around our house. Friends and family always comment on the fresh combination of asparagus, carrots, potatoes and chicken.

✓ **This tasty dish uses less sugar, salt and fat. Recipe includes *Diabetic Exchanges*.**

- 1/3 cup all-purpose flour
- 1/4 teaspoon paprika
- 4 boneless skinless chicken breast halves
- 1 tablespoon cooking oil
- 2 cups chicken broth, *divided*
- 1 teaspoon dill weed
- 3/4 teaspoon salt, optional
- 1/4 teaspoon dried basil
- 1/4 teaspoon pepper
- 4 medium potatoes, cut into bite-size pieces
- 3 medium carrots, cut into 2-inch pieces
- 1/2 pound fresh asparagus, cut into 2-inch pieces
- 2 tablespoons snipped fresh parsley

Combine the flour and paprika; set aside 2 tablespoons. Coat chicken in remaining mixture. In a skillet, brown chicken in oil over medium heat. Drain and set chicken aside. Combine 3/4 cup broth, dill, salt if desired, basil and pepper in the same skillet; bring to a boil. Add potatoes and carrots. Reduce heat; cover and simmer for 10 minutes. Add chicken; cook for 10 minutes. Add asparagus; cook 15-20 minutes or until chicken juices run clear and vegetables are tender. Combine reserved flour mixture and remaining broth; stir into skillet. Bring to a boil; cook and stir for 2 minutes or until slightly thickened. Sprinkle with parsley. **Yield:** 4 servings. **Diabetic Exchanges:** One serving (prepared without added salt) equals 3-1/2 lean meat, 2 starch, 1 vegetable; also, 362 calories, 479 mg sodium, 73 mg cholesterol, 38 gm carbohydrate, 35 gm protein, 8 gm fat.

Sesame Chicken
Mrs. Wilson Irey, Rochester Hills, Michigan

Cornflake crumbs and sesame seeds give these moist chicken breasts a crunchy golden coating.

- 1/2 cup dry bread crumbs
- 1/2 cup cornflake crumbs
- 3 tablespoons sesame seeds

> **SIZZLING SELECTIONS.** *Pictured at left, top to bottom: Harvest Chicken, Pepper Chicken and Rice (both recipes on this page) and Creamy Chicken Stew (recipe on page 40).*

- 1/2 teaspoon onion powder
- 1/4 teaspoon salt
- 1/8 teaspoon pepper
- 1/8 teaspoon garlic powder
- 1/2 cup buttermilk
- 4 boneless skinless chicken breast halves
- 3 tablespoons cooking oil

In a shallow bowl, combine the crumbs, sesame seeds, onion powder, salt, pepper and garlic powder. Pour buttermilk into another bowl. Pound chicken breasts to 1/4-in. thickness. Dip in buttermilk, then dredge in crumb mixture. In an electric skillet, heat oil to 350°. Fry chicken for 3-4 minutes per side or until browned and juices run clear. **Yield:** 4 servings.

Pepper Chicken and Rice
LaVonne Smith, Markle, Indiana
(PICTURED AT LEFT)

Besides being colorful and tasty, this dish has a nice variety of textures, like tender chicken and crunchy water chestnuts.

- 1-1/2 pounds boneless skinless chicken breasts, thinly sliced
- 1 cup chopped onion
- 1/4 cup cooking oil
- 1 cup uncooked long grain white rice
- 1 can (28 ounces) stewed tomatoes
- 1/2 cup soy sauce
- 1 tablespoon chicken bouillon granules
- 3/4 teaspoon salt-free herb and spice seasoning
- 1/2 teaspoon garlic powder
- 1/4 teaspoon cayenne pepper
- 1/2 teaspoon salt
- 2 medium green peppers, cut into 1-inch pieces
- 1 can (8 ounces) mushroom stems and pieces, drained
- 1 can (8 ounces) sliced water chestnuts, drained
- 2 tablespoons cornstarch
- 2 tablespoons water

In a large Dutch oven or wok, saute chicken and onion in oil over medium-high heat until chicken juices run clear. Add rice; cook and stir for 1 minute. Drain tomatoes, reserving liquid. Add enough water to make 2-1/4 cups. Add to pan along with soy sauce, bouillon and seasonings; bring to a boil. Reduce heat; cover and simmer for 15 minutes. Stir in green peppers and tomatoes. Cover and simmer for 5 minutes. Add mushrooms and water chestnuts; heat through. Combine cornstarch and water. Add to pan; cook and stir for 1 minute or until thickened and bubbly. **Yield:** 6 servings.

Creamy Chicken Stew
Nancy Renaut, Naperville, Illinois
(PICTURED ON PAGE 38)

My family spends hours outdoors…no matter what time of year. When we come in, we like nothing more than sitting down to warm biscuits topped with this steaming stew.

 2 tablespoons cooking oil
 3 pounds boneless skinless chicken breasts, cut into 1-inch cubes
 1 teaspoon *each* salt, pepper and paprika
 2 cups cubed peeled potatoes (1/2-inch pieces)
 3 large carrots, cut into 1/2-inch pieces
 2 cups frozen whole kernel corn
 1 cup *each* coarsely chopped green and sweet red pepper
 1 cup diced celery
 1 medium onion, diced
 2 teaspoons dried basil
 1 bay leaf
 1/4 teaspoon celery salt
 7 cups chicken broth, *divided*
 1/2 cup butter *or* margarine
 3/4 cup all-purpose flour
Warm biscuits

Heat oil in a Dutch oven; add chicken. Sprinkle with salt, pepper and paprika. Cook and stir until the chicken is browned; drain. Add vegetables, basil, bay leaf, celery salt and 5 cups broth; bring to a boil. Reduce heat; cover and simmer for 20 minutes or until potatoes and carrots are tender. Remove bay leaf. In a saucepan, melt butter; mix in flour. Cook and stir for 2 minutes or until smooth. Gradually whisk in remaining broth. Bring to a boil; cook and stir for 2 minutes or until thickened. Pour into the Dutch oven; bring to a boil. Reduce heat; simmer, uncovered, for 5 minutes or until heated through. Serve over biscuits. **Yield: 8-10 servings.**

Chicken with Ginger Sauce
Lynn Zukas, Spencer, Massachusetts

Life can be pretty busy on our dairy farm. So I favor foods that I can put on the table in no time. This dish is a hit at our house, even with our toddlers.

 2 boneless skinless chicken breast halves, cut into cubes
 3 tablespoons cooking oil, *divided*
 2 cups broccoli florets
 1 cup julienned carrots
 1 cup sliced fresh mushrooms
 1 cup fresh pea pods
 1/4 cup sliced green onions
 1/2 cup mayonnaise
 1/4 cup chicken broth
 1 garlic clove, minced
 1 tablespoon soy sauce
 1/2 teaspoon ground ginger
Hot cooked rice, optional
Sliced almonds, optional

In a large skillet or wok, stir-fry chicken in 1 tablespoon oil over medium-high heat for 5-7 minutes or until juices run clear. Remove chicken and set aside. In remaining oil, stir-fry broccoli, carrots, mushrooms, pea pods and onions for 8-10 minutes or until tender. Return chicken to skillet. Combine mayonnaise, broth, garlic, soy sauce and ginger; add to skillet. Reduce heat and cook until heated through. Serve over rice and sprinkle with almonds if desired. **Yield: 4 servings.**

Chicken 'n' Peppers
Cathy Zoller, Lovell, Wyoming
(PICTURED ON FRONT COVER)

With garden-fresh peppers and tender chicken, this dish is perfect when your family is craving a lighter dinner. Serve it with rice and a green salad.

✓ This tasty dish uses less sugar, salt and fat. Recipe includes *Diabetic Exchanges*.

 3/4 cup chicken broth
 1/4 cup soy sauce
 2 garlic cloves, minced
 2 tablespoons cornstarch
 3/4 teaspoon ground ginger
 1/4 teaspoon cayenne pepper
 6 boneless skinless chicken breast halves, cut into 1-inch pieces
 1 tablespoon cooking oil
 1 *each* medium green, yellow and sweet red peppers, cut into 1-inch pieces
 1/4 cup water

In a bowl, combine broth, soy sauce, garlic, cornstarch, ginger and cayenne pepper; mix well. Add chicken; stir to coat. Heat oil in a large skillet over medium-high heat. Add chicken; cook and stir constantly for 7 minutes. Reduce heat to medium. Add peppers and water; cook and stir for 5-8 minutes or until peppers are tender. **Yield: 6 servings. Diabetic Exchanges:** One serving (prepared with low-sodium chicken broth and soy sauce) equals 3 lean meat, 1 vegetable; also, 200 calories, 207 mg sodium, 73 mg cholesterol, 8 gm carbohydrate, 29 gm protein, 7 gm fat.

Cheesy Chicken and Asparagus
Adell Bennett, Lowville, New York

I was a cook at an elementary school where we had to use certain foods. But at home I got to experiment! My husband was—and still is—a tolerant taste-tester.

 2 boneless skinless chicken breast halves, cut into bite-size pieces
 1 tablespoon butter *or* margarine
 1 cup sliced fresh mushrooms
 3 green onions, sliced
 1 garlic clove, minced
 1 package (3 ounces) cream cheese
 1/4 teaspoon dried thyme
 1/4 teaspoon salt

1/8 teaspoon pepper
1 can (10-3/4 ounces) condensed cream of chicken soup, undiluted
1 can (5 ounces) evaporated milk
1 package (10 ounces) frozen chopped asparagus *or* broccoli
Hot cooked rice, optional

In a large skillet, saute chicken in butter for 5-6 minutes or until juices run clear. Stir in mushrooms, onions and garlic; saute for 3 minutes or until vegetables are tender. Cut cream cheese into cubes and stir into chicken mixture until melted. Add thyme, salt, pepper, soup and milk; stir to combine. Simmer, uncovered, for 10 minutes. Prepare asparagus or broccoli according to package directions; drain and stir into chicken mixture. Serve over rice if desired. **Yield:** 4 servings.

Favorite Skillet Dinner
Helen Purkerson, St. Helens, Oregon

This has been a family favorite for years. So when our children completed college and moved out on their own, this recipe went with them.

✓ This tasty dish uses less sugar, salt and fat. Recipe includes *Diabetic Exchanges*.

6 boneless skinless chicken breast halves
1 tablespoon olive *or* vegetable oil
1 tablespoon butter *or* margarine
3 medium potatoes, cut into 1-inch pieces
3 celery ribs, cut into 1-inch pieces
2 medium onions, cut into 1-inch pieces
1 package (16 ounces) frozen green beans
1 cup chicken broth
1/4 cup snipped fresh parsley
1 bay leaf
1 teaspoon salt, optional
1/2 teaspoon dried thyme
1/2 teaspoon pepper

In a skillet over medium heat, brown chicken in oil and butter for 10-12 minutes. Add remaining ingredients; stir to mix. Bring to a boil. Reduce heat; cover and simmer for 50-60 minutes or until vegetables are tender and chicken juices run clear. Remove bay leaf before serving. **Yield:** 6 servings. **Diabetic Exchanges:** One serving (prepared with margarine and low-sodium chicken broth and without added salt) equals 3 lean meat, 1 vegetable, 1 starch; also, 260 calories, 111 mg sodium, 73 mg cholesterol, 18 gm carbohydrate, 30 gm protein, 8 gm fat.

Asparagus-Lover's Stir-Fry
Nancy Street, Dublin, California

I find it a challenge to prepare vegetables so that they appeal to everyone...especially children. After tasting this special stir-fry, folks learn to love asparagus in no time.

4 tablespoons cooking oil, *divided*
1 cup sliced celery

4 cups fresh asparagus pieces
1/2 cup sliced green onions
4 boneless skinless chicken breast halves, cut into 1-inch strips
2 teaspoons grated orange peel
1 garlic clove, minced
1/2 cup water
2 tablespoons soy sauce
1/4 cup orange juice
2 tablespoons orange juice concentrate
4 teaspoons cornstarch
1/2 cup sliced almonds
Hot cooked rice

In a large skillet or wok, heat 2 tablespoons oil. Stir-fry celery over medium-high heat for 1 minute. Add asparagus and onions; stir-fry for 3-5 minutes or until asparagus is crisp-tender. Transfer to a bowl; set aside. Add remaining oil to the skillet. Stir-fry chicken, orange peel and garlic for 3-4 minutes or until chicken juices run clear. Combine water, soy sauce, orange juice, concentrate and cornstarch; add to skillet along with reserved vegetables. Cook and stir for 3 minutes or until sauce is thickened and vegetables are heated through. Stir in almonds. Serve over rice. **Yield:** 6-8 servings.

Hearty Chicken and Beans
Eva Greenman, Ida, Michigan

I had a can of chili beans in my pantry and decided to add it to one of my standby chicken recipes. I hope you enjoy the new and interesting taste.

3-1/2 to 4 pounds chicken thighs
1/2 cup soy sauce, *divided*
2 tablespoons brown sugar
1 garlic clove, minced
1/2 teaspoon ground cumin, optional
2 tablespoons cooking oil
2 celery ribs, thinly sliced
1 can (15 ounces) spicy chili beans, undrained
1 can (8 ounces) sliced water chestnuts, drained
1 can (4 ounces) mushroom stems and pieces, drained
1-1/4 cups water
3 tablespoons cornstarch
Hot cooked rice

Bone and skin chicken; cut into bite-size pieces. In a shallow bowl or large resealable plastic bag, combine 1/4 cup soy sauce, brown sugar, garlic and cumin if desired; add chicken. Cover or close bag and refrigerate for 4 hours or overnight. Drain chicken, discarding marinade. In a large skillet, heat oil over medium-high. Cook chicken for 6-8 minutes or until juices run clear. Remove chicken with a slotted spoon; set aside. Saute celery in drippings for 2 minutes or until crisp-tender. Add beans, water chestnuts and mushrooms; cook for 5 minutes or until heated through. Add chicken. Mix water, cornstarch and remaining soy sauce; stir into chicken mixture. Bring to a boil; cook and stir for 2 minutes or until thickened. Serve over rice. **Yield:** 6-8 servings.

Chicken 'n' Dumplings with Sour Cream Gravy

Doris Butler, Burbank, Illinois
(PICTURED AT LEFT)

This recipe has been in my family for years. My mother, who is of Czech descent, made this saucy chicken when I was a child. Now my daughters make it for their own families.

- 1 cup all-purpose flour
- 3 teaspoons paprika, *divided*
- 2 teaspoons salt
- 5 pounds broiler-fryer chicken pieces
- 1/4 cup butter *or* margarine
- 1/2 cup *each* chopped celery, onion and green pepper
- 2-1/2 cups chicken broth

DUMPLINGS:
- 1-1/4 cups all-purpose flour
- 1-1/2 teaspoons baking powder
- 1/2 teaspoon salt
- 1 egg
- 1/2 cup milk

GRAVY:
- 2 tablespoons cornstarch
- 2 tablespoons water
- 1 cup (8 ounces) sour cream
- 2 tablespoons minced fresh parsley

Combine flour, 2 teaspoons of paprika and salt; dredge chicken. Brown in a Dutch oven in butter, a few pieces at a time. Remove and set aside. In the same pan, saute celery, onion and green pepper until tender. Add broth, chicken and remaining paprika. Cover and simmer for 45 minutes or until chicken juices run clear. Remove chicken to a serving platter and keep warm. For dumplings, combine flour, baking powder and salt. Beat egg and milk; stir into flour mixture and mix well. Drop dough, 2 tablespoonfuls at a time, into simmering broth. Cover and simmer for 10 minutes. Remove dumplings to platter and keep warm. For gravy, combine cornstarch and water; stir into broth. Bring to a boil; cook for 2 minutes. Reduce heat; add sour cream and parsley. Serve with chicken and dumplings. **Yield:** 6 servings.

Chicken Sausage Saute

Susan Lynn Hauser, Etters, Pennsylvania
(PICTURED AT LEFT)

A good friend gave me this recipe years ago. Since then, I've made it for weekday dinners, special occasions and potlucks. It always disappears quickly.

- 4 medium potatoes (about 1-1/2 pounds), peeled and cut into 1-inch pieces
- 1 pound Italian sausage, cut into 1-inch pieces

> **HUNGRY FOR COUNTRY?** *Pictured at left, top to bottom: Chicken Sausage Saute and Chicken 'n' Dumplings with Sour Cream Gravy (both recipes on this page).*

Cooking oil, optional
- 3 boneless skinless chicken breast halves, cut into 1-inch pieces
- 1 *each* large green pepper, sweet red pepper and onion, cut into 1-inch pieces
- 1 package (10 ounces) frozen green beans, thawed
- 1/2 cup water
- 1 teaspoon dried oregano
- 3/4 teaspoon salt
- 1/4 teaspoon pepper

In a large skillet over medium heat, brown potatoes and sausage in oil if desired for 15-20 minutes. Add chicken, peppers and onion; saute for 15 minutes or until chicken is browned. Add beans, water, oregano, salt and pepper. Reduce heat; cover and simmer for 15 minutes or until vegetables are tender. **Yield:** 6 servings.

Cola Chicken

Jean Jarvis, Wautoma, Wisconsin

Everyone who tries this chicken asks for the recipe. They're surprised to hear that soda is the secret ingredient!

- 1 can (12 ounces) diet cola
- 1/2 cup ketchup
- 2 to 4 tablespoons minced onion
- 1/4 teaspoon dried oregano
- 1/4 teaspoon garlic powder
- 8 chicken pieces, skin removed

In a large skillet, combine first five ingredients. Bring to a boil; boil for 1 minute. Add chicken; stir to coat. Reduce heat to medium; cover and simmer for 20 minutes. Uncover and simmer for 45 minutes or until chicken juices run clear. **Yield:** 4 servings.

Eggplant Provencale

Sharon Skildum, Maple Grove, Minnesota

This hearty one-dish meal is sure to please. The classic combination of chicken, eggplant and pasta is unbeatable.

- 3 cups peeled eggplant strips
- 1/4 cup butter *or* margarine
- 1/2 cup chopped onion
- 1/2 cup sliced celery
- 1 garlic clove, minced
- 2 cups cubed cooked chicken
- 1 can (8 ounces) tomato sauce
- 1 tablespoon dried parsley flakes
- 1 teaspoon dried basil
- 1 teaspoon dried oregano
- 1 teaspoon salt
- 1/8 teaspoon pepper
- 2 cups cooked pasta
- 1/2 cup shredded mozzarella cheese

In a large skillet over medium heat, saute eggplant in butter for 10 minutes. Add the onion, celery and garlic; saute until vegetables are tender. Add the next seven ingredients; simmer for 10 minutes. Stir in pasta; sprinkle with mozzarella cheese. **Yield:** 4-6 servings.

Dilly Chicken and Potatoes
Genevieve Kirmis, Bismarck, North Dakota

When our sons were growing up, sitting around the table and enjoying good meals like this was a family pastime. That tradition continues whenever they come to visit.

- 1 broiler-fryer chicken (3-1/2 to 4 pounds), cut up
- 1 pound new potatoes, cut into chunks
- 2 tablespoons cooking oil
- 1 cup half-and-half cream
- 1 to 1-1/2 teaspoons salt
- 1/2 teaspoon seasoned pepper
- 3/4 cup sliced green onions
- 1/4 cup snipped fresh dill *or* 1 tablespoon dill weed
- 1/2 cup sour cream

In a large skillet over medium heat, brown chicken and potatoes in oil for 10-15 minutes. Remove chicken and potatoes; set aside. Discard all but 1 tablespoon drippings. To drippings, add cream, salt and pepper; stir to mix. Return chicken and potatoes to skillet. Sprinkle with onions and dill. Cover and simmer for 50-60 minutes or until chicken juices run clear and potatoes are tender. With a slotted spoon, remove chicken and potatoes to a serving platter; keep warm. Add sour cream to pan; stir to mix and heat through. Serve with chicken and potatoes. **Yield:** 4-6 servings.

Chicken and Tomato Scampi
Jan Gridley, Elverson, Pennsylvania

My mother always had a knack for turning ordinary ingredients into "lively" meals. Now, I try to do the same. Of course, nothing can compare to Mom's meals!

✓ This tasty dish uses less sugar, salt and fat. Recipe includes *Diabetic Exchanges*.

- 2 to 3 garlic cloves, minced
- 1/4 cup chopped green onions
- 2 tablespoons butter *or* margarine
- 1 tablespoon olive *or* vegetable oil
- 4 boneless skinless chicken breast halves, cut into 1-inch pieces
- 1 teaspoon salt, optional
- 1/2 teaspoon pepper
- 1 can (14-1/2 ounces) Italian stewed tomatoes
- 1/4 cup lemon juice
- 1/2 teaspoon sugar
- 2 teaspoons cornstarch
- 2 teaspoons cold water
- 1/4 cup chopped fresh parsley

Hot cooked rice, optional

In a skillet over medium heat, saute garlic and onions in butter and oil until onions are tender. Add chicken, salt if desired and pepper. Cook for 6-8 minutes or until chicken juices run clear. Add tomatoes, lemon juice and sugar; heat through. Combine cornstarch and water; stir into chicken mixture. Bring to a boil; cook and stir for 1 minute or until thickened. Add parsley. Serve over rice if desired. **Yield:** 4 servings. **Diabetic Exchanges:** One serving (prepared with margarine and without added salt and served without rice) equals 3 lean meat, 1-1/2 vegetable, 1 fat; also, 255 calories, 356 mg sodium, 73 mg cholesterol, 8 gm carbohydrate, 28 gm protein, 13 gm fat.

Picante Chicken
Mary Henken, Alma, Illinois

I came up with this recipe after eating a similar dish in a Mexican restaurant. My family enjoys this chicken's slightly spicy flavor...I like its ease of preparation.

✓ This tasty dish uses less sugar, salt and fat. Recipe includes *Diabetic Exchanges*.

- 4 boneless skinless chicken breast halves, cubed
- 1 tablespoon cooking oil
- 1 cup chopped onion
- 1 cup chopped celery
- 1 cup chopped green *or* sweet red pepper
- 1 jar (12 ounces) picante sauce
- 1/2 teaspoon lemon pepper seasoning
- 1/4 teaspoon salt, optional

Hot cooked rice, optional

In a large skillet or wok, saute chicken in oil for 10-12 minutes or until juices run clear. Add onion, celery and pepper; saute until crisp-tender. Add picante sauce, lemon pepper and salt if desired; simmer for 30 minutes. Serve over rice if desired. **Yield:** 4 servings. **Diabetic Exchanges:** One serving (prepared without added salt and served without rice) equals 3 lean meat, 2 vegetable; also, 229 calories, 929 mg sodium, 73 mg cholesterol, 12 gm carbohydrate, 28 gm protein, 7 gm fat.

Chicken a la King
Carma DeGroot, Arlington, Washington

We raise fryers to feed our family for months. And this is one of our favorite ways to prepare chicken. It's a traditional dish that's sure to please.

- 1/2 cup chopped onion
- 1/4 cup butter *or* margarine
- 1/4 cup all-purpose flour
- 3/4 teaspoon salt
- 1/2 teaspoon pepper
- 1/4 teaspoon dried sage
- 1-1/2 cups milk
- 1 cup chicken broth
- 2 cups sliced fresh mushrooms
- 1 cup sliced carrots, cooked
- 1 cup peas, cooked
- 1/2 cup green pepper, cooked
- 2 cups cubed cooked chicken

Warm biscuits

In saucepan, saute onion in butter until tender. Add the flour, salt, pepper and sage; stir to form a smooth paste. Gradually add milk and broth, stirring constantly. Bring to a boil; cook an additional minute or until thickened. Add vegetables and chicken; heat through. Serve over biscuits. **Yield:** 4-6 servings.

Chicken Piccata
Linda Carver, Cedar Rapids, Iowa

I first fixed this chicken for guests during the Christmas season. It was a refreshing change from turkey and ham. Now this is a special supper in our home throughout the year.

- 1/2 cup all-purpose flour
- 1/2 teaspoon garlic powder
- 1/2 teaspoon paprika
- 2 eggs
- 6 tablespoons lemon juice, *divided*
- 4 boneless skinless chicken breast halves
- 1/2 cup butter *or* margarine
- 2 teaspoons chicken bouillon granules
- 1 cup water

In a small bowl, combine flour, garlic powder and paprika; set aside. In another bowl, beat eggs and 2 tablespoons lemon juice. Dip chicken pieces in egg mixture, then roll in flour mixture. In a large skillet over medium-high heat, brown chicken in butter. Combine bouillon, water and remaining lemon juice; pour over chicken. Cover and simmer for 20 minutes or until juices run clear. **Yield:** 4 servings.

Chicken Stew with Dumplings
Elizabeth Durance, Sarnia, Ontario

My mother usually didn't care for dumplings. But she raved about this stew...dumplings and all. It's a down-home delicious meal that I make often for my family.

- 2-1/2 to 3 pounds chicken thighs *or* legs
- 5 cups water
- 1 teaspoon salt
- 1/2 teaspoon pepper
- 1/2 teaspoon dried basil
- 1/4 teaspoon dried thyme
- 3/4 pound new potatoes, quartered
- 3 carrots, cut into 2-inch pieces
- 2 celery ribs, sliced
- 1 medium onion, cut into eighths
- 1 package (10 ounces) frozen peas

DUMPLINGS:
- 1-1/2 cups all-purpose flour
- 2 teaspoons baking powder
- 1/2 teaspoon salt
- 3 tablespoons butter *or* margarine
- 3/4 cup milk
- 1/4 cup minced fresh parsley

Place chicken and water in a 5-qt. Dutch oven. Cover and cook over medium heat for 1 to 1-1/2 hours or until chicken is tender. Skim fat. Remove chicken from broth; allow to cool. Debone chicken and cut into chunks; return to broth. Add next nine ingredients. Cover and cook over medium heat for 15-20 minutes or until vegetables are tender. Meanwhile, combine flour, baking powder and salt in a bowl; cut in butter until mixture resembles coarse crumbs. Stir in milk and parsley. Drop dough by rounded tablespoonfuls into simmering stew. Cook, uncovered, for 10 minutes. Cover and cook for 8-10 minutes or until the dumplings are tender. **Yield:** 8 servings.

Mediterranean Chicken
Sally Hinton, Liverpool, Pennsylvania

I learned to cook with a Mediterranean flair while living in Israel. You'll find this chicken captures that wonderful warm-weather taste.

- 1 broiler-fryer chicken (3-1/2 to 4 pounds), cut up
- 3 tablespoons cooking oil, *divided*
- 3 medium onions, thinly sliced
- 3 garlic cloves, minced
- 1/4 cup chopped fresh parsley
- 1 tablespoon chopped fresh tarragon *or* 1 teaspoon dried tarragon
- 1 teaspoon salt
- 1/2 teaspoon pepper
- 1 cup chopped stuffed olives

Hot cooked rice *or* noodles

In a large skillet over medium heat, brown chicken in 2 tablespoons oil. Remove chicken and set aside. Add remaining oil to skillet. Saute onions and garlic until tender. Add parsley, tarragon, salt and pepper; mix well. Return chicken to skillet; cover with onion mixture. Sprinkle with olives. Reduce heat; cover and simmer 40-45 minutes or until chicken is tender and juices run clear. Serve over rice or noodles. **Yield:** 4-6 servings.

Broccoli Barley Saute
Michelle Tolzman, Chaska, Minnesota

Here's a fun way to "spice up" your skillet suppers! Barley is a nice change of pace from rice, and the veggies and peanuts add a fun and festive crunch.

✓ **This tasty dish uses less sugar, salt and fat. Recipe includes** *Diabetic Exchanges*.

- 1/2 cup quick-cooking barley
- 1/3 cup water
- 3 tablespoons soy sauce
- 2 teaspoons cornstarch
- 1 garlic clove, minced
- 1 tablespoon cooking oil
- 2 carrots, thinly sliced
- 2 cups fresh broccoli florets
- 2 green onions, sliced
- 2 cups diced cooked chicken
- 1/2 cup unsalted peanuts, optional

Prepare barley according to package directions. In a small bowl, combine water, soy sauce and cornstarch; set aside. In a large skillet or wok, saute garlic in oil for 15 seconds. Add carrots; stir-fry for 1 minute. Add broccoli and onions; stir-fry for 2-3 minutes. Stir in soy sauce mixture; simmer and stir for 1 minute or until thickened. Add chicken and barley; heat through. Stir in peanuts if desired. **Yield:** 6 servings. **Diabetic Exchanges:** One serving (prepared with low-sodium soy sauce and without peanuts) equals 1 starch, 1 lean meat, 1 vegetable; also, 149 calories, 273 mg sodium, 28 mg cholesterol, 18 gm carbohydrate, 11 gm protein, 4 gm fat.

A HARVEST OF FRESH IDEAS. *Clockwise from top left: Chicken and Peas with Pasta, Quick Skillet Chicken, Honey Lime Chicken, Easy Chicken Creole and Chicken Italiano (all recipes on pages 48 and 49).*

Chicken and Peas with Pasta
Mrs. Delane Mason, Wamego, Kansas

(PICTURED ON PAGE 46)

This creamy noodle dinner has a savory, satisfying flavor that just says "home". Unfortunately, everyone likes it so much there are never any leftovers!

       4 boneless skinless chicken breast halves, cut
            into 1-inch pieces
       2 tablespoons cooking oil
    1/2 cup chopped onion
       1 medium green *or* sweet red pepper, chopped
       1 garlic clove, minced
       2 cups frozen peas
       1 cup chicken broth
       1 cup half-and-half cream
       2 teaspoons Italian seasoning
Salt to taste
       8 ounces pasta, cooked and drained
    1/2 cup grated Parmesan cheese
       1 cup coarsely chopped walnuts, toasted

In a 5-qt. Dutch oven, saute chicken in oil over medium heat until browned. Add onion, pepper and garlic; saute until tender. Add peas, broth, cream, Italian seasoning and salt; bring to a boil. Reduce heat; simmer for 10 minutes. Add pasta and Parmesan cheese; simmer for 5 minutes. Garnish with walnuts. **Yield:** 4-6 servings.

Quick Skillet Chicken
LaVonne Elsbernd, Fortuna, North Dakota

(PICTURED ON PAGE 47)

Our teenagers' many activities keep me going right up until dinnertime. So I welcome foods like this that can be made in a hurry. Plus it's a great way to use leftover chicken.

       3 cups diced cooked chicken
       1 egg, beaten
    1/2 cup crushed saltines
    1/2 cup ground almonds
    1/2 teaspoon salt
       3 tablespoons butter *or* margarine
       1 cup sliced celery
       2 medium tomatoes, cut into thin wedges
    1/2 medium green pepper, julienned
    1/2 cup sugar
       3 tablespoons cornstarch
    1/2 cup water
    1/2 cup lemon juice
       1 can (6 ounces) pineapple juice
       2 tablespoons soy sauce
Hot cooked rice
Chow mein noodles

In a bowl, combine chicken and egg. Add saltines, almonds and salt; toss well. In a skillet, saute chicken mixture in butter over medium heat for 10 minutes, stirring occasionally. Add vegetables; saute for 2-3 minutes or until crisp-tender. Remove from the heat and set aside. In a saucepan, combine sugar and cornstarch; add water, juices and soy sauce. Stir until smooth. Bring to a boil over medium heat; boil for 1 minute or until thickened. Pour over chicken and vegetables; heat through. Serve with rice and chow mein noodles. **Yield:** 6 servings.

Honey Lime Chicken
Faye Hoffman, Dubuque, Iowa

(PICTURED ON PAGE 47)

Everyone in the family enjoys the delightful flavors of this tart, sweet chicken. I usually round out the meal with rice, salad and dessert.

       4 boneless skinless chicken breast halves
    1-1/2 teaspoons garlic salt
       1 tablespoon cooking oil
       1 can (20 ounces) pineapple slices
    1/4 cup honey
       3 tablespoons fresh lime juice
       2 tablespoons soy sauce
       2 teaspoons cornstarch
Grated peel of 1 lime

Sprinkle chicken with garlic salt. In a large skillet, brown chicken in oil over medium-high heat. Drain pineapple, reserving juice. Add 1/4 cup juice to skillet; reserve remaining juice. Cover and simmer for 6-8 minutes or until chicken juices run clear. Remove to a serving platter; keep warm. In a small bowl, combine honey, lime juice, soy sauce, cornstarch and reserved pineapple juice; pour into skillet. Bring to a boil over medium heat, stirring for 1-2 minutes. Add pineapple; heat through. Pour over chicken; sprinkle with lime peel. Serve immediately. **Yield:** 4 servings.

Easy Chicken Creole
Maxine Weaver, Petersburg, West Virginia

(PICTURED ON PAGE 46)

While I was growing up, my family spent time in Haiti, where we enjoyed eating many authentic dishes such as this. It's now a meal my husband requests often.

       1 cup sliced celery
       1 cup diced green pepper
       1 cup chopped onion
       2 garlic cloves, minced
    1/4 cup cooking oil
    1/4 cup all-purpose flour
       5 cups chicken broth
       6 cups cubed cooked chicken
       2 cans (6 ounces *each*) tomato paste
    1/4 cup chopped fresh parsley
       4 teaspoons Worcestershire sauce
       2 teaspoons lemon juice
       1 teaspoon salt
    1/2 teaspoon *each* pepper, sugar and dried thyme
      12 to 16 drops hot pepper sauce
Hot cooked rice

In a large skillet over medium heat, saute celery, green pepper, onion and garlic in oil until tender. Add flour; cook and stir for 5 minutes or until browned. Stir in broth.

Bring to a boil; cook and stir for 2 minutes. Add remaining ingredients except rice. Return to a boil. Reduce heat; cover and simmer for 10 minutes or until heated through. Serve over rice. **Yield:** 8-10 servings.

Chicken Italiano

Donna Aho, Fargo, North Dakota

(PICTURED ON PAGE 46)

As a working mom, I'm always thrilled to find foods that suit our busy life-style. This recipe from my mother-in-law is frequently on our weekday menus.

    4 boneless skinless chicken breast halves
1/2 teaspoon salt
1/4 teaspoon pepper
    2 eggs, lightly beaten
3/4 cup Italian-seasoned bread crumbs
    1 to 2 tablespoons butter *or* margarine
    1 to 2 tablespoons cooking oil
    1 garlic clove, minced
1/2 cup chicken broth
    2 tablespoons lemon juice

Flatten chicken to 1/4-in. thickness; sprinkle with salt and pepper. Dip into eggs, then coat with crumbs. In a large skillet, heat butter and oil. Saute chicken and garlic over medium heat, turning chicken once, for 12-15 minutes or until juices run clear. Remove to a serving platter; keep warm. Add broth and lemon juice to skillet; simmer for 2-3 minutes or until volume is reduced by half. Spoon over chicken. **Yield:** 4 servings.

Ginger Chicken Stir-Fry

Bonnie Gilbertson, Merrillan, Wisconsin

We like hot spicy foods, so we always add the highest amount of cayenne pepper called for here. No matter how much you use, this dish has just the right amount of pizzazz!

✓ This tasty dish uses less sugar, salt and fat. Recipe includes *Diabetic Exchanges.*

    4 boneless skinless chicken breast halves, cut
       into bite-size pieces
    2 tablespoons cooking oil
    2 cups *each* broccoli florets, cauliflowerets and
       carrot pieces
    1 cup bite-size onion pieces
    2 cups chicken broth
1/4 cup teriyaki sauce
1/4 cup soy sauce
1/4 cup cold water
    3 tablespoons cornstarch
1/2 teaspoon pepper
1/2 teaspoon ground ginger
1/8 to 1/4 teaspoon cayenne pepper
    1 garlic clove, minced

In a large skillet or wok, stir-fry chicken in oil over medium-high heat for 10 minutes or until juices run clear. Remove chicken and set aside. In the same skillet, stir-fry broccoli, cauliflower, carrot and onion for 5-8 minutes or until tender. Combine remaining ingredients; add to

the skillet. Bring to a boil; cook and stir for 2 minutes or until thickened. Return chicken to skillet and heat through. **Yield:** 8 servings. **Diabetic Exchanges:** One serving (prepared with low-sodium chicken broth and soy sauce) equals 2 lean meat, 2 vegetable; also, 151 calories, 655 mg sodium, 37 mg cholesterol, 10 gm carbohydrate, 16 gm protein, 5 gm fat.

Chicken with Cucumber Sauce

Sheryl Ann Houghton, Spring Grove, Pennsylvania

I've served this chicken to nearly all our friends and relatives, and it's been met with many "Mmmms!" I sometimes prepare extra sauce to serve over steamed fresh carrots.

    1/4 cup yellow cornmeal
1-1/2 teaspoons dry mustard
    1/4 teaspoon ground nutmeg
    1/8 to 1/4 teaspoon cayenne pepper
    1/2 teaspoon Old Bay seasoning, optional
      8 boneless skinless chicken breast halves
      2 tablespoons cooking oil
CUCUMBER SAUCE:
      1 bottle (8 ounces) ranch salad dressing
      1 cup diced peeled cucumber
      1 tablespoon sliced green onion
    1/2 teaspoon dill weed

Combine cornmeal, mustard, nutmeg, cayenne pepper and Old Bay seasoning if desired; coat chicken. In a skillet over medium heat, cook chicken for 5-7 minutes on each side or until browned and juices run clear. Meanwhile, combine sauce ingredients in a saucepan; cook over low heat until heated through. Serve over chicken. **Yield:** 8 servings. **Editor's Note:** Chicken may also be served as a sandwich on buns topped with warm or chilled cucumber sauce.

Chicken Pilaf Saute

Dorothy Schmidt, Falun, Alberta

I like to see how much I can "dress up" leftovers as an exciting new meal. Here's a flavorful combination that I often serve guests when I'm short on time.

    2 cups cubed cooked chicken
    1 cup uncooked long grain rice
1/4 cup chopped onion
    3 tablespoons butter *or* margarine
    3 chicken bouillon cubes
2-1/2 cups boiling water
1/2 teaspoon salt
1/2 teaspoon dried thyme
1/4 teaspoon pepper
    1 cup chopped fresh tomatoes
1/2 cup slivered almonds, toasted

In a skillet over medium heat, saute chicken, rice and onion in butter for 10 minutes. Dissolve bouillon in water. Add salt, thyme and pepper; stir to mix. Pour into skillet; bring to a boil. Reduce heat; cover and simmer for 15 minutes. Stir in tomatoes and almonds. Cover and cook for 15-20 minutes or until rice is tender. **Yield:** 2-4 servings.

Chicken and Corn Medley
Lisa Jensen, Waupaca, Wisconsin
(PICTURED AT LEFT)

I usually make this in the summer when all the vegetables are fresh from our garden. My family loves the "zip" in this dish …I like the fact that they're getting a wholesome meal.

- 3/4 cup all-purpose flour
- 2 teaspoons salt, *divided*
- 3/4 teaspoon pepper, *divided*
- 4 boneless skinless chicken breast halves, thinly sliced
- 2 tablespoons cooking oil
- 1-1/2 cups chopped onion
- 2 cups sliced fresh mushrooms
- 2 tablespoons lemon juice
- 3 garlic cloves, minced
- 2 cups chicken broth
- 1 tablespoon Dijon mustard
- 2 tablespoons minced fresh basil *or 2 teaspoons dried basil*
- 3/4 teaspoon dried oregano
- 1/8 teaspoon cayenne pepper
- 2 cups fresh *or* frozen corn
- 2 cups seeded chopped tomatoes
- 1 medium green pepper, julienned
- 1/2 cup chopped fresh parsley

Hot cooked noodles *or* rice, optional

In a large bowl, combine flour, 1 teaspoon salt and 1/2 teaspoon pepper. Add chicken and toss to coat. In a large skillet, heat oil over medium heat. Saute chicken until browned; remove and set aside. In the drippings, saute onion until tender. Toss mushrooms with lemon juice. Add mushrooms and garlic to the skillet; cook and stir for 4 minutes or until tender. Add the broth, remaining salt and pepper, mustard, basil, oregano, cayenne pepper and chicken. Simmer, uncovered, for 15 minutes. Stir in the corn, tomatoes and green pepper; simmer for 10 minutes. Sprinkle with parsley. Serve over noodles or rice if desired. **Yield:** 6 servings.

Garlic-Brown Sugar Chicken
Florence Yuriy, Shortdale, Manitoba

My family always asks me to save some of this cooked chicken so that I can make Garlic Chicken Fried Rice (next recipe) for dinner the next night!

- 1 broiler-fryer chicken (3-1/2 to 4 pounds), cut up
- 1 cup packed brown sugar
- 2/3 cup vinegar
- 1/4 cup lemon-lime soda
- 2 to 3 tablespoons minced garlic cloves
- 2 tablespoons soy sauce
- 1 teaspoon pepper

FARE WITH FLAIR. *Pictured at left: Chicken and Corn Medley (recipe on this page).*

Place chicken in a 13-in. x 9-in. x 2-in. glass baking dish or large resealable plastic bag. Combine remaining ingredients; pour over chicken. Cover or close bag and refrigerate 2-4 hours. Transfer chicken and marinade to a large skillet; bring to a boil. Reduce heat; cover with lid ajar and simmer 45 minutes or until juices run clear. **Yield:** 4 servings.

Garlic Chicken Fried Rice
Florence Yuriy, Shortdale, Manitoba

This fried rice uses leftover chicken (see the Garlic-Brown Sugar Chicken recipe on this page). So it's perfect when you need a quick and easy meal on busy weekdays.

- 1 egg
- 1/4 cup cooking oil, *divided*
- 1 cup sliced celery
- 2 to 3 garlic cloves, minced
- 6 cups cold cooked rice
- 1 cup diced fully cooked ham
- 1 to 2 cups chopped leftover Garlic-Brown Sugar Chicken (recipe on this page) *or* cooked chicken
- 1/2 cup soy sauce
- 1 teaspoon pepper
- 1/4 to 1/2 teaspoon ground ginger

In a large skillet or wok, scramble egg in 1 tablespoon oil, breaking into small pieces. Remove from skillet and set aside. Add remaining oil to skillet; stir-fry celery and garlic over medium-high heat until crisp-tender. Add rice; cook, stirring constantly, for 3 minutes. Stir in ham, chicken, soy sauce, pepper, ginger and egg; heat through. **Yield:** 4-6 servings.

South Seas Skillet
Carol Mead, Los Alamos, New Mexico

When I was younger, my mother and 4-H sparked my interest in cooking. Outside of the kitchen, you'll find me working on a craft, at a church function or in the garden.

- 4 boneless skinless chicken breast halves, cut into thin strips
- 1/4 cup butter *or* margarine
- 1/3 cup sliced green onions
- 3 garlic cloves, minced
- 1 cup water
- 1/3 cup raisins
- 3 tablespoons chopped fresh parsley, *divided*
- 2 teaspoons brown sugar
- 1 teaspoon chicken bouillon granules
- 1/8 teaspoon salt
- 1 orange, cut into 8 wedges

Hot cooked rice

In a large skillet, saute chicken in butter for 6-8 minutes or until juices run clear. Remove from skillet; set aside. Saute onions and garlic in drippings until tender. Add water, raisins, 2 tablespoons parsley, brown sugar, bouillon and salt. Simmer for 15 minutes or until liquid is reduced by half. Add chicken and heat through. Sprinkle with remaining parsley. Squeeze juice from orange wedges over chicken. Serve over rice. **Yield:** 4 servings.

Stir-Fried Chicken Fajitas
Nancy Zimmerer, Medina, Ohio

When we're in the mood for Mexican food, I'll reach for this recipe. Much of the meal can be prepared in advance, so I can avoid the last-minute rush at dinnertime.

- 1/4 **cup vegetable oil**
- 3 **tablespoon red wine vinegar**
- 1-1/2 **teaspoons sugar**
- 1-1/2 **teaspoons chili powder**
- 1 **teaspoon dried oregano**
- 1/2 **teaspoon garlic powder**
- 1/2 **teaspoon salt**
- 1/4 **teaspoon pepper**
- 1-1/2 **pounds boneless skinless chicken breasts, cut into thin strips**
- 8 **flour tortillas (10 inches), warmed**
- 2 **cups shredded lettuce**
- 2 **cups (8 ounces) shredded cheddar** *or* **Monterey Jack cheese**
- 1 **large tomato, diced**
- 3/4 **cup sour cream**

Taco sauce

In a glass bowl or resealable plastic bag, mix first eight ingredients. Add chicken; toss to coat. Cover or close bag and refrigerate for 4 hours. Drain, discarding marinade. Saute chicken in a large skillet over medium heat for 6-7 minutes or until juices run clear. Spoon about 1/2 cup chicken down the center of each tortilla. Top with lettuce, cheese, tomato, sour cream and taco sauce. Fold in sides of tortilla and serve immediately. **Yield:** 8 servings.

Spicy Chicken Saute
Polly Wankum, Oswego, Illinois

Whenever our daughters come home from college, this is the dish they always request. My husband enjoys it so much I usually prepare it a couple of times a month.

✓ **This tasty dish uses less sugar, salt and fat. Recipe includes** *Diabetic Exchanges.*

- 2 **boneless skinless chicken breast halves, julienned**
- 2 **tablespoons cooking oil,** *divided*
- 1 **celery rib, sliced**
- 1 **medium carrot, julienned**
- 1 **medium green pepper, julienned**
- 1/4 **cup chicken broth**
- 1 **tablespoon soy sauce**
- 1/2 **teaspoon salt, optional**
- 1/2 **teaspoon cornstarch**
- 1/4 to 1/2 **teaspoon crushed red pepper flakes**
- 1/4 **teaspoon hot pepper sauce**

Hot cooked rice, optional

In a skillet over medium-high heat, saute chicken in 1 tablespoon oil for 5-7 minutes or until juices run clear. Remove chicken and set aside. Saute celery, carrot and green pepper in remaining oil for 5-7 minutes or until tender. Return chicken to pan. Combine broth, soy sauce, salt if desired, cornstarch, red pepper flakes and hot pepper sauce; add to skillet. Bring to a boil; cook for 1 minute

to thicken. Serve over rice if desired. **Yield:** 4 servings. **Diabetic Exchanges:** One serving (prepared with low-sodium chicken broth and soy sauce, without added salt and served without rice) equals 1-1/2 lean meat, 1 vegetable, 1 fat; also, 154 calories, 180 mg sodium, 37 mg cholesterol, 5 gm carbohydrate, 15 gm protein, 9 gm fat.

Skillet Chicken and Vegetables
Annette Phillips, Baton Rouge, Louisiana

My mother-in-law and sisters-in-law put together a cookbook containing my husband's favorite meals when we got married. This stir-fry is one of the recipes in the book.

- 2 **tablespoons cooking oil**
- 1 **broiler-fryer chicken (3-1/2 to 4 pounds), cut up**
- 1 **cup sliced onion**
- 1 **can (10-3/4 ounces) condensed cream of celery soup, undiluted**
- 2 **tablespoons Worcestershire sauce**
- 1/2 to 1 **teaspoon salt**
- 1/2 **teaspoon dried oregano**
- 2 **cups sliced zucchini**
- 1 **package (10 ounces) frozen green beans, thawed**

In a large skillet, heat oil over medium-high heat. Brown chicken, a few pieces at a time; remove from skillet and set aside. Discard all but 2 teaspoons drippings. Saute onion in drippings until tender. Add soup, Worcestershire sauce, salt and oregano; stir until smooth. Add chicken; bring to a boil. Reduce heat; cover and simmer for 30-40 minutes. Add zucchini and green beans; cover and simmer for 10 minutes or until chicken juices run clear. **Yield:** 4 servings.

Sweet-and-Sour Chicken
Michelle Scarborough, Prescott Valley, Arizona

My husband and I moved to the country 10 years ago, and I love it! We keep busy with daily chores, so I appreciate quick and easy meals like this.

- 3 **tablespoons all-purpose flour**
- 1/2 **teaspoon garlic powder**
- 1/2 **teaspoon salt**
- 1/2 **teaspoon pepper**
- 6 **boneless skinless chicken breast halves, cut into 1-inch cubes**
- 3 **tablespoons cooking oil,** *divided*
- 3 **celery ribs, sliced**
- 2 **medium green peppers, diced**
- 1 **medium onion, diced**
- 1/2 **cup ketchup**
- 1/2 **cup lemon juice**
- 1/2 **cup crushed pineapple with syrup**
- 1/3 **cup packed brown sugar**

Hot cooked rice

Combine flour, garlic powder, salt and pepper; coat chicken. In a skillet over medium-high heat, saute chicken in 2 tablespoons oil for 8-10 minutes or until tender.

Remove and set aside. Saute celery, green peppers and onion in remaining oil for 5 minutes or until crisp-tender. Return chicken to pan. Combine ketchup, lemon juice, pineapple and brown sugar; add to skillet. Bring to a boil; cook an additional minute or until heated through. Serve over rice. **Yield:** 6 servings.

Broccoli Stir-Fry
Mary Newsom, Grand Ridge, Florida

I clipped this recipe out of a newspaper years ago and it's since become a family favorite. I like to serve it with fresh fruit and warm homemade bread.

✓ This tasty dish uses less sugar, salt and fat. Recipe includes *Diabetic Exchanges.*

      1 pound boneless skinless chicken breasts,
        cut into thin strips
      2 tablespoons cooking oil
      1 small onion, julienned
      2 cups fresh broccoli florets
      1 medium green pepper, julienned
      1 garlic clove, minced
  1-1/2 cups vegetable juice
      2 tablespoons soy sauce
      1 tablespoon cornstarch
  1-1/2 teaspoons brown sugar
    1/2 teaspoon ground ginger

In a large skillet or wok, stir-fry chicken in oil for 7 minutes or until juices run clear; remove and set aside. In the same skillet, stir-fry onion until tender. Add broccoli, green pepper and garlic; stir-fry until tender. In a small bowl, combine remaining ingredients until smooth; pour over vegetable mixture. Add chicken; bring to a boil. Cook and stir for 1 minute or until sauce is thickened and bubbly. **Yield:** 4 servings. **Diabetic Exchanges:** One serving (prepared with low-sodium soy sauce) equals 3 lean meat, 3 vegetable, 1 fat; also, 276 calories, 488 mg sodium, 79 mg cholesterol, 14 gm carbohydrate, 30 gm protein, 12 gm fat.

Easy Fried Rice
Lori Schweer, Mapleton, Minnesota

This recipe really captures the flavor of fried rice served in restaurants. Use leftover chicken and rice for a satisfying meal that's easy to put together.

      2 eggs, beaten
    1/4 teaspoon salt
      3 tablespoons cooking oil, *divided*
      4 cups cooked rice
  1-1/2 cups frozen oriental blend vegetables
    1/2 cup sliced green onions
      1 garlic clove, minced
      1 cup diced cooked chicken
      3 tablespoons soy sauce
      1 tablespoon chicken broth
    1/2 teaspoon pepper
    1/4 teaspoon ground ginger
      4 bacon strips, cooked and crumbled

Combine eggs and salt. In a large skillet or wok over medium heat, scramble eggs in 1 teaspoon oil, breaking into small pieces. Remove from skillet and set aside. Add remaining oil to skillet. Stir-fry rice over medium-high heat for 5 minutes. Add vegetables, onions and garlic; stir-fry for 5 minutes. Add chicken; stir-fry for 3-5 minutes or until heated through. Combine soy sauce, broth, pepper and ginger. Add to rice; stir to coat. Add bacon and eggs; heat through. **Yield:** 4 servings.

Smothered Ginger Chicken
Iva Smith, Wilmington, Massachusetts

Liven up ordinary chicken with this simple, saucy skillet dish. No one in my family can resist the moist chicken and old-fashioned gravy.

    1/2 cup plus 3 tablespoons all-purpose flour, *divided*
  1-1/2 teaspoons salt, *divided*
    1/4 teaspoon pepper
      1 broiler-fryer chicken (3-1/2 to 4 pounds), cut up
      3 tablespoons cooking oil
      1 cup chopped onion
    1/4 cup *each* chopped green and sweet red pepper
      3 garlic cloves, minced
    1/2 teaspoon ground ginger
      3 cups chicken broth

Combine 1/2 cup flour, 1 teaspoon salt and pepper; coat chicken pieces. Heat oil in a large skillet; fry chicken, a few pieces at a time, until well browned. Remove from skillet and set aside. Add onion, peppers and garlic to drippings; saute until tender. Stir in ginger and remaining flour and salt; cook for 2 minutes. Add chicken broth; bring to a boil. Cook 2-3 minutes or until thickened and bubbly. Add chicken; cover tightly and simmer for 45 minutes or until chicken juices run clear. **Yield:** 4 servings.

Western Drumsticks
Doris Heath, Bryson City, North Carolina

With baked beans, corn and green pepper, these juicy drumsticks are a meal by themselves. But I like to serve them with a green salad and fresh bread.

      1 can (16 ounces) barbecue-flavored baked
        beans, undrained
      1 can (8 ounces) whole kernel corn, drained
  1-1/2 cups chopped green pepper
      1 tablespoon ketchup
      4 chicken legs, skin removed

In a 2-qt. saucepan, combine beans, corn, green pepper and ketchup; add chicken legs. Cover and simmer, stirring occasionally, for 40 minutes or until chicken juices run clear. **Yield:** 2 servings.

> **QUICK COOKING.** When using leftover chicken in a stir-fry recipe, add it to the skillet last and cook just long enough to heat through.

Oven Entrees

There's no better way to call your family to the table than with the aromatic flavors of these down-home roasts, baked dishes, quiches—and even pizzas!

Sweet Smoky Chicken Legs
Jane MacKinnis, Eden, Maryland
(PICTURED AT LEFT)

When we crave the taste of barbecued chicken in the middle of winter, this oven-baked version hits the spot! You'll love the short list of ingredients.

    2 medium onions, sliced
    3 pounds chicken legs
1-1/2 to 2 teaspoons hickory smoked salt
  1/2 cup ketchup
  1/2 cup maple syrup
  1/4 cup vinegar
    2 tablespoons prepared mustard

Place onions in greased 13-in. x 9-in. x 2-in. baking dish; arrange chicken in a single layer over onions. Sprinkle with salt. Combine remaining ingredients and pour over all, completely coating chicken. Bake, uncovered, at 350° for 1 hour or until juices run clear, basting several times. **Yield:** 4-6 servings.

Asparagus-Pecan Quiche
Nancy Horsburgh, Everett, Ontario
(PICTURED AT LEFT)

This egg dish was created at the spur of the moment when my son wanted quiche one morning. I used whatever ingredients I had on hand, and this was the delicious result.

    1 unbaked pastry shell (9 inches)
    1 cup cut fresh *or* frozen asparagus (2-inch pieces)
1-1/4 cups (5 ounces) shredded Swiss cheese
    1 cup chopped cooked chicken
  1/2 cup chopped pecans, *divided*
  1/4 cup chopped onion
    1 tablespoon all-purpose flour
1-1/2 cups half-and-half cream
    3 eggs, beaten
    1 teaspoon Dijon mustard
  1/2 teaspoon salt
    3 drops hot pepper sauce
    2 tablespoons grated Parmesan cheese

Line unpricked pastry shell with a double thickness of heavy-duty aluminum foil. Bake at 450° for about 8 minutes or until edges just begin to brown. Remove from oven and discard foil. Set crust aside. Place asparagus in a small saucepan with enough water to cover; cook until crisp-tender. Drain thoroughly; toss with Swiss cheese, chicken, 1/4 cup pecans, onion and flour. Spoon into baked crust. Combine cream, eggs, mustard, salt and hot pepper sauce; pour over asparagus mixture. Sprinkle with Parmesan cheese. Top with remaining pecans. Bake at 350° for 35-40 minutes or until a knife inserted near the center comes out clean. Let stand 5 minutes before cutting. **Yield:** 6-8 servings.

Simply Great Chicken
Carolyn Casteel, Glendale, Arizona
(PICTURED AT LEFT)

I know you'll love this baked chicken…it's easy to prepare as well as tasty. So even on the busiest days, you can still serve your family a hearty dinner.

    1 broiler-fryer chicken (3-1/2 to 4 pounds),
      cut up and skin removed
    1 envelope (.7 ounce) Italian salad dressing mix
  1/2 cup packed brown sugar

In a greased 13-in. x 9-in. x 2-in. baking dish, place chicken in a single layer. Sprinkle with salad dressing mix and sugar. Bake, uncovered, at 350° for 55-60 minutes or until juices run clear. **Yield:** 4 servings.

Orange Chicken
Irma Collison, Pigeon, Michigan

This chicken has a fresh and fruity citrus flavor that is sure to satisfy your family. I've been asked to make this more times than I can remember!

✓ This tasty dish uses less sugar, salt and fat. Recipe includes *Diabetic Exchanges*.

    1 broiler-fryer chicken (3-1/2 to 4 pounds), cut
      up and skin removed
    1 can (6 ounces) frozen orange juice
      concentrate, thawed
    2 teaspoons lemon juice
    1 teaspoon chicken bouillon granules
    1 teaspoon ground savory
  1/2 teaspoon ground sage
  1/2 teaspoon salt, optional

Place chicken pieces in a greased 13-in. x 9-in. x 2-in. baking dish. Combine orange juice, lemon juice, bouillon, savory, sage and salt if desired; pour over chicken. Bake, uncovered, at 350° for 60-70 minutes or until juices run clear, basting occasionally. **Yield:** 4 servings. **Diabetic Exchanges:** One serving (prepared without added salt) equals 2-1/2 lean meat, 2 fruit; also, 253 calories, 74 mg sodium, 62 mg cholesterol, 30 gm carbohydrate, 24 gm protein, 4 gm fat.

DELIGHTFULLY FILLING. *Pictured at left, top to bottom: Sweet Smoky Chicken Legs, Asparagus-Pecan Quiche and Simply Great Chicken (all recipes on this page).*

Roasted Chicken with Sausage Stuffing

Julie Ann Schmidt, Aurora, Illinois
(PICTURED ON FRONT COVER)

This roasted chicken not only has a down-home country flavor, it's attractive as well. Friends and family are always impressed when I put this on the table.

- 1/2 pound bulk pork sausage
- 1/2 cup chopped onion
- 1/2 cup chopped celery
- 1/2 cup diced sweet red pepper
- 1 tablespoon butter *or* margarine
- 5 cups unseasoned stuffing croutons
- 1/4 cup minced fresh parsley
- 1-1/2 teaspoons minced fresh tarragon *or* 1/2 teaspoon dried tarragon
- 1 teaspoon poultry seasoning
- 1/2 teaspoon salt
- 1/4 teaspoon pepper
- 1-1/2 to 2 cups chicken broth, *divided*
- 1 roasting chicken (6 to 7 pounds)

In a medium skillet, cook sausage, onion, celery and red pepper in butter until sausage is no longer pink and vegetables are crisp-tender; do not drain. Place croutons in a large bowl; add sausage mixture. Stir in the parsley, tarragon, poultry seasoning, salt and pepper. Stir in enough broth until stuffing is moistened and holds together. Just before baking, loosely stuff into chicken. Place with breast side up on a shallow rack in a roasting pan. Pour 1/2 cup broth around chicken. Bake, uncovered, at 325° for 2-1/2 to 3 hours or until juices run clear, basting occasionally. **Yield:** 6 servings.

Chicken-Mushroom Loaf

Pearl Altman, Spring Church, Pennsylvania

We began restoring our 1860 farmhouse when we bought it 40 years ago...and we still have projects on our list! After a hard day's work, it's nice to sit down to this chicken loaf.

✓ This tasty dish uses less sugar, salt and fat. Recipe includes *Diabetic Exchanges.*

- 1 can (10-3/4 ounces) condensed cream of mushroom soup, undiluted
- 2/3 cup milk
- 2 eggs, lightly beaten
- 3 cups cubed cooked chicken
- 1 cup cooked rice
- 1 cup dry bread crumbs
- 1 jar (2 ounces) chopped pimientos, drained
- 1 teaspoon onion salt, optional
- 1 teaspoon celery seed
- 1/2 teaspoon salt, optional
- 1/2 teaspoon paprika
- 1/4 teaspoon pepper

In a large bowl, combine soup, milk and eggs; stir until well mixed. Add all remaining ingredients and mix well. Pour into a greased 8-in. x 4-in. x 2-in. loaf pan. Bake, uncovered, at 325° for 50-55 minutes. Let stand 10 minutes before serving. **Yield:** 6 servings. **Diabetic Exchanges:** One serving (prepared with reduced-fat soup and without onion salt and salt) equals 2 lean meat, 1-1/2 starch; also, 232 calories, 329 mg sodium, 117 mg cholesterol, 26 gm carbohydrate, 18 gm protein, 6 gm fat.

Cheesy Chicken Roll-Ups

Sally Uhrmacher, Nelson, Nebraska

Until I served my family these slightly spicy chicken breasts, they never cared for white meat. Now they prefer them to dark meat...and to just about anything else I make!

- 8 large boneless skinless chicken breast halves
- 1 block (6 ounces) cheddar cheese
- 1 cup crushed cheddar cheese crackers (about 2 cups whole crackers)
- 4-1/2 teaspoons taco seasoning mix
- 1/4 cup butter *or* margarine, melted

Pound chicken breasts to 1/4-in. thickness. Cut cheese into eight 3-1/2-in. x 3/4-in. sticks. Place one cheese stick in the center of each chicken breast. Fold long sides over cheese; fold ends up and secure with a toothpick if necessary. In a bowl, combine crackers and taco seasoning. Dip chicken in butter, then roll in crumb mixture. Place, seam side down, in a greased 13-in. x 9-in. x 2-in. baking dish. Cover and bake at 400° for 20-25 minutes or until chicken is no longer pink. **Microwave Directions:** Place chicken rolls in a greased 13-in. x 9-in. x 2-in. microwave-safe baking dish. Cover with waxed paper and microwave on high for 5 minutes. Turn each roll; cover and microwave on high for 4-5 minutes or until chicken is no longer pink. This recipe was tested in a 700-watt microwave. **Yield:** 8 servings.

Chicken Potpie

Brenda Sawatzky, Niverville, Manitoba

Chicken potpie was a favorite childhood food, but my mother never wrote the recipe down. After some trial and error, I came up with this version. It tastes just like hers!

- 1 cup chopped celery
- 1/4 cup chopped onion
- 2 tablespoons butter *or* margarine
- 2-1/4 cups water, *divided*
- 1-1/2 cups diced cooked chicken
- 1 cup frozen mixed vegetables
- 3/4 cup uncooked thin egg noodles
- 1 tablespoon chicken bouillon granules
- 1/4 teaspoon pepper
- 2 tablespoons cornstarch

Pastry for single-crust pie (10 inches)

In a medium saucepan, saute celery and onion in butter until tender. Add 2 cups water, chicken, vegetables, noodles, bouillon and pepper. Cook, uncovered, over medium heat for 5 minutes or just until noodles are tender, stirring occasionally. Combine cornstarch and remaining water; add to saucepan. Increase heat to high; cook, stirring constantly, for 2 minutes or until thickened and bubbly. Pour into an ungreased 10-in. pie plate. Roll out pastry to fit plate; place over filling. Cut several 1-in. slits in the top. Bake at 350° for 45-55 minutes or until lightly browned. Let stand for 5 minutes before serving. **Yield:** 6 servings.

Asparagus Supreme
Betty Teegarden, Polo, Missouri

My husband and I enjoy spending time in the kitchen and trying new recipes. It's fun to create new dishes...especially when they're as successful as this one.

- 3 cups cooked rice
- 1 teaspoon salt, *divided*
- 3/4 teaspoon pepper, *divided*
- 1 package (12 ounces) frozen cut asparagus, thawed and drained
- 4 boneless skinless chicken breast halves, cut into 1-inch strips
- 1/4 cup cooking oil
- 1 cup sliced fresh mushrooms
- 6 green onions, chopped
- 1/4 cup chopped sweet red pepper
- 1 can (10-3/4 ounces) condensed cream of mushroom soup, undiluted
- 1/2 cup mayonnaise
- 2 teaspoons lemon juice
- 1 teaspoon salt-free seasoning blend
- 1/2 cup shredded cheddar cheese

Spread rice in a greased 11-in. x 7-in. x 2-in. baking dish. Sprinkle with 1/2 teaspoon salt and 1/4 teaspoon pepper. Cover with asparagus. Sprinkle chicken with remaining salt and pepper. In a large skillet, cook chicken in oil over medium-high heat until browned on all sides. With a slotted spoon, remove chicken and place over asparagus. Add mushrooms, onions and red pepper to skillet; saute until tender. Spoon over chicken. Combine soup, mayonnaise, lemon juice and seasoning blend; spread over vegetables. Sprinkle with cheese. Cover and bake at 350° for 40-45 minutes. **Yield:** 6 servings.

Harvest Vegetable Bake
Janet Weisser, Seattle, Washington

This delicious dish is packed with a large assortment of vegetables. Served with a green salad, it makes an excellent entree.

- 2-1/2 to 3 pounds skinless chicken thighs
- 2 bay leaves
- 4 small red potatoes, cut into 1-inch pieces
- 4 small onions, quartered
- 4 small carrots, cut into 2-inch pieces
- 2 celery ribs, cut into 2-inch pieces

- 2 small turnips, cut into 1-inch pieces
- 1 medium green pepper, cut into 1-inch pieces
- 12 small fresh mushrooms
- 2 teaspoons salt
- 1 teaspoon dried rosemary
- 1/2 teaspoon pepper
- 1 can (14-1/2 ounces) diced tomatoes with liquid

Place chicken in a greased 13-in. x 9-in. x 2-in. baking dish; add bay leaves. Top with potatoes, onions, carrots, celery, turnips, green pepper and mushrooms. Sprinkle with salt, rosemary and pepper. Pour tomatoes over all. Cover and bake at 375° for 1-1/2 hours or until chicken juices run clear and vegetables are tender. Remove bay leaves before serving. **Yield:** 6-8 servings.

COOL RULE. Never refrigerate a stuffed chicken, whether it's cooked or uncooked. The stuffing should always be refrigerated in a separate container.

Veggie-Stuffed Pizza Bread
Dawn Lofthus, Olney, Maryland

I made this pizza bread for my son's first birthday party, and needless to say, it was a hit. Each guest left with their own little "present"—this recipe!

- 2 cups frozen vegetable blend (carrots, cauliflower, asparagus and broccoli)
- 1/2 cup chopped onion
- 1 garlic clove, minced
- 1 tablespoon olive *or* vegetable oil
- 1/2 cup half-and-half cream
- 1 package (3 ounces) cream cheese, cubed
- 1 cup diced cooked chicken
- 1 tablespoon dried parsley flakes
- 1/2 teaspoon dried basil
- 1/4 teaspoon celery salt
- 1/4 teaspoon pepper
- 5 tablespoons grated Parmesan cheese, *divided*
- 1/2 cup shredded mozzarella cheese, *divided*
- Additional oil and basil
- 1 can (10 ounces) refrigerated pizza crust dough

Cook vegetables according to package directions; drain. Cut larger vegetables into bite-size pieces; set aside. In a medium saucepan, saute onion and garlic in oil until tender. Add cream and cream cheese; cook over low heat, stirring constantly, until smooth. Stir in chicken, parsley, basil, celery salt and pepper; heat through. Add 4 tablespoons Parmesan cheese and 1/4 cup mozzarella cheese. Stir until cheese melts; remove from the heat. Brush baking sheet with additional oil. Roll out pizza crust onto baking sheet, keeping the rectangular shape. Brush crust with oil. Sprinkle remaining mozzarella cheese lengthwise down center. Spoon the chicken mixture over the cheese, spreading it about 4 in. wide. Moisten edges of dough. Fold the long sides over the chicken mixture and pinch to seal. Pinch ends to seal and fold under. Brush the top with oil; sprinkle with basil and remaining Parmesan. Bake at 425° for 10-12 minutes or until top is golden brown. Serve immediately. **Yield:** 4-6 servings.

Vegetable Chicken

Dorothy McGrew Hood, Northbrook, Illinois
(PICTURED AT LEFT)

The original recipe for this dish only called for vegetables, but I eventually added the chicken to make it a mouth-watering main meal.

✓ This tasty dish uses less sugar, salt and fat. Recipe includes *Diabetic Exchanges*.

  1 broiler-fryer chicken (3-1/2 to 4 pounds), cut up and skin removed
  2 cups sliced celery
  2 cups fresh *or* frozen cut green beans
1-1/2 cups sliced carrots
  1 large onion, sliced
  1 small zucchini, diced
  1 can (14-1/2 ounces) diced tomatoes with liquid
  3 tablespoons quick-cooking tapioca
  1 tablespoon sugar
  2 teaspoons salt, optional
1/2 teaspoon pepper

In an ungreased 13-in. x 9-in. x 2-in. baking dish, place chicken, celery, green beans, carrots and onion. In a small bowl, combine zucchini, tomatoes, tapioca, sugar, salt if desired and pepper. Pour over chicken and vegetables. Cover tightly and bake at 350° for 1-1/2 hours or until chicken juices run clear and vegetable mixture thickens. Stir vegetables occasionally during baking. **Yield:** 4 servings. **Diabetic Exchanges:** One serving (prepared without added salt) equals 3 lean meat, 3 vegetable; also, 242 calories, 298 mg sodium, 62 mg cholesterol, 27 gm carbohydrate, 25 gm protein, 4 gm fat.

Sweet-and-Sour Baked Chicken

Marion Skildum, St. Paul, Minnesota
(PICTURED AT LEFT)

This is one of my favorite entrees to make for company. It's assembled the night before and popped into the oven before guests arrive, so there's plenty of time to visit.

  1 cup soy sauce
  1 cup water
3/4 cup sugar
1/2 cup vegetable oil
1/2 cup white wine vinegar
  1 can (6 ounces) pineapple juice
1-1/2 teaspoons ground ginger
  1 teaspoon salt
3/4 to 1 teaspoon garlic powder
 12 broiler-fryer chicken pieces (3-1/2 to 4 pounds)

In a large resealable plastic bag or a glass 13-in. x 9-in. x 2-in. baking dish, combine first nine ingredients. Add chicken pieces; turn to coat. Cover or close bag and refrigerate 8 hours or overnight. Drain, discarding all but 1

---

cup marinade. Place chicken in a 15-in. x 10-in. x 1-in. baking pan; add reserved marinade. Bake, uncovered, at 350° for 1-1/4 hours or until juices run clear. **Yield:** 6-8 servings.

Baked Chicken with Mushroom Gravy

Cathy Young, Guelph, Ontario

I have frequently served this chicken to my single friends who don't like to cook for themselves. It always gets rave reviews.

1/4 cup butter *or* margarine, melted
1/4 cup all-purpose flour
  1 broiler-fryer chicken (3-1/2 to 4 pounds), cut up
  2 cups sliced onions
  4 ounces fresh mushrooms, sliced
  1 can (10-3/4 ounces) condensed cream of mushroom soup, undiluted
  1 can (5 ounces) evaporated milk
  1 cup (4 ounces) shredded cheddar cheese
1/2 teaspoon salt
1/8 teaspoon pepper
Dash paprika
Hot cooked rice, optional

Pour melted butter into an ungreased 13-in. x 9-in. x 2-in. baking dish; set aside. Place flour in a large resealable plastic bag. Add chicken, a few pieces at a time; shake to coat. Place chicken, skin side down, in baking dish. Bake, uncovered, at 425° for 30 minutes. Turn chicken pieces; bake an additional 20 minutes. Meanwhile, saute onions and mushrooms in a nonstick skillet until tender. In a bowl, combine next five ingredients. Drain and discard chicken drippings. Cover chicken with onions, mushrooms and the soup mixture. Sprinkle with paprika. Reduce heat to 325°. Cover and bake for 20 minutes or until juices run clear. Serve over rice if desired. **Yield:** 4 servings.

Sunshine Chicken

Janis Garrett, Macon, Georgia

I love sweet-and-sour flavoring and came up with this version to capture that taste in chicken. The gelatin and mustard make an attractive golden sauce.

  1 package (3 ounces) lemon-flavored gelatin
  3 tablespoons butter *or* margarine, melted
  3 tablespoons prepared mustard
  2 teaspoons garlic salt
1/4 teaspoon pepper
  4 large boneless skinless chicken breast halves
  2 tablespoons thinly sliced almonds
Hot cooked rice, optional

In a small bowl, combine gelatin, butter, mustard, garlic salt and pepper. Brush over both sides of the chicken breasts and place in an ungreased 11-in. x 7-in. x 2-in. baking dish. Spoon remaining mixture around chicken. Cover and bake at 350° for 20-25 minutes, basting once. Uncover; baste and sprinkle with almonds. Bake, uncovered, 15 minutes longer or until juices run clear. Serve over rice if desired. **Yield:** 4 servings.

OVEN-FRESH FAVORITES. *Pictured at left, top to bottom: Vegetable Chicken and Sweet-and-Sour Baked Chicken (both recipes on this page).*

Zesty Chicken and Rice
Ella West, Lake Charles, Louisiana

A dear friend gave me this recipe years ago. Italian dressing and seasoning add just the right amount of "zip" to ordinary chicken and rice.

✓ **This tasty dish uses less sugar, salt and fat. Recipe includes** *Diabetic Exchanges*.

    6 chicken breast halves (bone in)
  1/3 cup Italian salad dressing
    1 can (14-1/2 ounces) chicken broth
    1 bag (16 ounces) frozen broccoli, carrots and
      water chestnuts
  2/3 cup uncooked long grain rice
1-1/4 teaspoons Italian seasoning

Place chicken in a greased 13-in. x 9-in. x 2-in. baking dish. Pour dressing over chicken. Bake, uncovered, at 400° for 20 minutes. Combine broth, vegetables, rice and Italian seasoning; pour over chicken. Cover and bake at 350° for 30 minutes. Uncover; bake 30 minutes more or until chicken juices run clear and rice is tender. **Yield:** 6 servings. **Diabetic Exchanges:** One serving (prepared with low-fat dressing and low-sodium broth) equals 3 lean meat, 1 starch, 1 vegetable; also, 266 calories, 208 mg sodium, 73 mg cholesterol, 21 gm carbohydrate, 31 gm protein, 6 gm fat.

Italian-Style Supper
Lucille Sardegna, Port Alsworth, Alaska

I make this chicken quite often for my family. The whole house is filled with a wonderful aroma from the garlic and Parmesan cheese while it's baking.

    8 small red potatoes, thinly sliced
    1 teaspoon salt
    1 broiler-fryer chicken (3-1/2 to 4 pounds), cut
      up and skin removed
  3/4 cup grated Parmesan cheese
  1/2 cup minced fresh parsley
    1 to 2 garlic cloves, minced
  1/2 to 1 teaspoon pepper

Place potatoes in a greased 13-in. x 9-in. x 2-in. baking dish; sprinkle with salt. Arrange chicken over potatoes. Combine Parmesan cheese, parsley, garlic and pepper; sprinkle over chicken. Cover and bake at 350° for 60-70 minutes or until chicken juices run clear and potatoes are tender. **Yield:** 4-6 servings.

Chicken and Broccoli Quiche
Naomi Giddis, Grawn, Michigan

This is a nice change of pace from traditional quiches because it uses ground chicken. I like to make both pies and freeze one for an already-made meal later on.

    1 pound ground chicken*
  1/2 cup chopped onion
    2 packages (10 ounces *each*) frozen chopped
      broccoli, thawed and well drained
    2 unbaked pastry shells (9 inches)
    1 can (10-3/4 ounces) condensed cheddar
      cheese soup, undiluted
  3/4 cup milk
    6 eggs, lightly beaten
  1/2 teaspoon salt
  1/4 teaspoon dried thyme
  1/4 teaspoon pepper

In a saucepan, brown chicken and onion; drain. Stir in broccoli. Divide among pie shells. In a small bowl, mix remaining ingredients. Pour over chicken mixture in each pie shell. Bake, uncovered, at 350° for 35-40 minutes or until a knife inserted near the center comes out clean. Let stand for 5 minutes before cutting. **Yield:** 12-16 servings. ***Editor's Note:** Ground chicken may be found in many grocery stores. Or you may finely chop chicken in a food processor or meat grinder.

Bacon and Blue Cheese Chicken
Jane MacKinnis, Eden, Maryland

This area of Maryland is considered "poultry country", so we see a lot of recipes calling for chicken. I hope this recipe becomes as popular in your home as it is in mine!

    3 tablespoons dried minced onion
    2 tablespoons dried parsley flakes
    2 teaspoons dried basil
    1 teaspoon poppy seeds
    8 chicken thighs
    1 cup chunky blue cheese salad dressing
    6 bacon strips, cooked and crumbled

In a small bowl, combine onion, parsley, basil and poppy seeds; rub over chicken. Place in an ungreased 11-in. x 7-in. x 2-in. baking dish. Pour dressing over chicken. Bake, uncovered, at 350° for 40 minutes. Sprinkle with bacon. Return to the oven for 5-10 minutes or until juices run clear. **Yield:** 6-8 servings.

Chicken Rice Balls
Katy Martin, Toledo, Oregon

Here's a fun way to serve two delicious staples—chicken and rice. Topped with the creamy mushroom sauce, these are one of my husband's favorite foods.

  1/2 cup finely chopped celery
  1/3 cup sliced green onions, *divided*
    2 tablespoons butter *or* margarine
    2 tablespoons all-purpose flour
  1/2 cup chicken broth
    2 cups cooked rice
1-1/2 cups finely chopped cooked chicken
  1/2 cup shredded cheddar cheese
    1 egg, lightly beaten
  1/2 teaspoon salt
  1/2 teaspoon chili powder
  1/4 teaspoon poultry seasoning
  1/2 cup finely crushed cornflakes

1 can (10-3/4 ounces) condensed cream of mushroom soup, undiluted
1/4 cup milk

In a medium saucepan, saute celery and half of the onions in butter until tender. Stir in flour. Add broth; cook and stir for 2 minutes (mixture will be thick). Stir in rice, chicken, cheese, egg, salt, chili powder and poultry seasoning until well mixed. Shape 1/4 cupfuls into balls. Roll each in cornflake crumbs and place in a greased 13-in. x 9-in. x 2-in. baking dish. Bake, uncovered, at 350° for 25-30 minutes. Meanwhile, in a saucepan, combine soup, milk and remaining onions. Cook and stir over medium heat until smooth and heated through; serve over balls. **Yield:** 4-6 servings.

Orange-Coated Chicken
Paulette Reyenga, Brantford, Ontario

This delightfully different dish was in the first cookbook I used as a new bride. My guests commented on the fruity flavor, which made me feel proud of my accomplishment!

2 eggs
1/3 cup orange juice
1 cup seasoned bread crumbs
1 teaspoon paprika
1 teaspoon salt
1 teaspoon grated orange peel
1 broiler-fryer chicken (3-1/2 to 4 pounds), cut up
1/4 cup butter *or* margarine, melted
Orange slices
2 tablespoons minced fresh parsley

In a shallow bowl, beat eggs and orange juice. In another bowl, mix bread crumbs, paprika, salt and orange peel. Dip chicken pieces in egg mixture, then in crumb mixture. Place, skin side down, in a greased 13-in. x 9-in. x 2-in. baking dish; drizzle with butter. Bake, uncovered, at 400° for 30 minutes. Turn chicken; bake at 350° for 20 minutes. Top with orange slices and sprinkle with parsley. Return to the oven for 5-10 minutes or until juices run clear. **Yield:** 4 servings.

30-Minute Chicken
John Kosmas, Minneapolis, Minnesota

I like to help out in the kitchen whenever I can. This one-pan meal is great when entertaining because it can be prepared in a hurry and bakes in no time.

✓ This tasty dish uses less sugar, salt and fat. Recipe includes *Diabetic Exchanges.*

1 medium onion, sliced
4 boneless skinless chicken breast halves
1/2 teaspoon salt, optional
1/4 teaspoon pepper
1/2 pound fresh mushrooms, sliced
2 medium zucchini, sliced
2 garlic cloves, minced
1 can (14-1/2 ounces) diced tomatoes with liquid
3/4 teaspoon dried basil

1/2 teaspoon dried oregano
Grated Parmesan cheese, optional

In a greased 13-in. x 9-in. x 2-in. baking dish, place onion and chicken breasts; sprinkle with salt if desired and pepper. Layer mushrooms and zucchini over chicken. Combine garlic, tomatoes, basil and oregano; pour over vegetables. Cover tightly. Bake at 450° for 30 minutes or until juices run clear. Sprinkle with Parmesan cheese if desired. **Yield:** 4 servings. **Diabetic Exchanges:** One serving (prepared without added salt and Parmesan) equals 3 lean meat, 2 vegetable; also, 212 calories, 331 mg sodium, 73 mg cholesterol, 15 gm carbohydrate, 30 gm protein, 4 gm fat.

Peach-Glazed Chicken
Mary Knauer, Erlanger, Kentucky

Preparing this tasty glaze is a great way to have kids help in the kitchen because it's quick and easy. As much as our kids like to cook, they like taste-testing even better!

1 broiler-fryer chicken (3-1/2 to 4 pounds), cut up
1 jar (4 ounces) strained peaches (baby food)
1/3 cup packed brown sugar
1/3 cup ketchup
1/3 cup vinegar
1 tablespoon soy sauce
1/2 teaspoon ground ginger
1 teaspoon salt
1/4 teaspoon garlic powder
1/4 teaspoon pepper

Place chicken in a single layer in a greased or foil-lined 13-in. x 9-in. x 2-in. baking dish. Bake, uncovered, at 350° for 20 minutes. Combine remaining ingredients; pour over chicken. Bake, uncovered, for an additional 45 minutes or until juices run clear. **Yield:** 4 servings.

Tropical Chicken Bake
Jane Bower, Normal, Illinois

Cooking is a wonderful way to let your creativity come through. I start with basic recipes, then add my own personal touches. My family is always happy with the results!

4 boneless skinless chicken breast halves
1 tablespoon butter *or* margarine
3 medium sweet potatoes, cooked, peeled and quartered
2 medium firm bananas, cut into 1/2-inch slices
1 can (11 ounces) mandarin oranges, drained
1 can (8 ounces) crushed pineapple, drained
1/2 cup sweet-and-sour sauce
1/3 cup chopped almonds *or* pecans

In a skillet over medium heat, brown chicken in butter on both sides. In an ungreased 2-qt. baking dish, combine sweet potatoes, bananas, oranges and pineapple. Top with chicken; pour sauce over all. Sprinkle with nuts. Bake, uncovered, at 350° for 20-25 minutes or until juices run clear. **Yield:** 4 servings.

DINNER TABLE STAPLES. *Clockwise from top right: Roasted Chicken with Brown Gravy, Key Lime Chicken Thighs, Chicken and Pepperoni Pizza, Broccoli-Chicken Cups and Chicken Mozzarella (all recipes on page 64).*

Chicken and Pepperoni Pizza

Diana Messner, Livonia, Michigan

(PICTURED ON PAGE 62)

My husband is the supreme pizza maker in the family. He'll try new ingredient combinations and stick with the winners. This palate-pleasing pizza is one of his "masterpieces"!

      1 package (16 ounces) prebaked Italian bread shell crust
  3/4 cup pizza sauce
      1 cup frozen cut broccoli, cooked and drained
      1 cup cubed cooked chicken
      1 can (4 ounces) mushroom stems and pieces, drained
  1/4 cup sliced pepperoni
      8 small cherry tomatoes, halved
1-1/2 cups (6 ounces) shredded mozzarella cheese

Place crust on a lightly greased pizza pan. Spread with pizza sauce. Top with the broccoli, chicken, mushrooms, pepperoni and tomatoes. Sprinkle with cheese. Bake at 400° for 15-20 minutes or until heated through. **Yield:** 6-8 servings.

Broccoli-Chicken Cups

Shirley Gerber, Roanoke, Illinois

(PICTURED ON PAGE 62)

I first sampled these when my cousin made them for a bridal shower. All the ladies raved over the fantastic flavor of their individual "casseroles".

      2 tubes (10 ounces *each*) refrigerated biscuit dough
      2 cups (8 ounces) shredded cheddar cheese, *divided*
1-1/3 cups crisp rice cereal
      1 cup cubed cooked chicken
      1 can (10-3/4 ounces) condensed cream of mushroom soup, undiluted
      1 package (10 ounces) frozen chopped broccoli, cooked and drained

Place biscuits in greased muffin cups, pressing dough over the bottom and up the sides. Add 1 tablespoon cheese and cereal to each cup. Combine chicken, soup and broccoli; spoon into cups. Bake at 375° for 20-25 minutes or until bubbly. Sprinkle with remaining cheese. **Yield:** 10-12 servings.

Roasted Chicken with Brown Gravy

Annie Tompkins, Deltona, Florida

(PICTURED ON PAGE 63)

Folks say this is one of the most delicious roasted chickens they've ever had. There's only one problem—there are never any leftovers!

      1 teaspoon dried thyme *or* rosemary, crushed
      1 teaspoon salt
  1/2 teaspoon pepper
  1/2 teaspoon paprika
      1 broiler-fryer chicken (3-1/2 to 4 pounds)
      3 bacon strips
      1 cup beef broth
  1/4 cup cold water
      1 tablespoon all-purpose flour

Combine thyme or rosemary, salt, pepper and paprika; rub on outside of chicken and in cavity. Place on a rack in a shallow roasting pan. Arrange bacon strips over breast portion of chicken. Bake, uncovered, at 450° for 15 minutes. Add broth to pan; baste chicken with broth. Reduce heat to 350°. Bake, basting several times, for 1-1/4 hours or until juices run clear. Remove chicken and keep warm. Skim off excess fat from pan juices. Combine water and flour; stir into juices. Bring to a boil, stirring constantly; cook and stir for 1 minute or until thickened. If desired, crumble bacon into gravy. Serve with chicken. **Yield:** 4-6 servings. **Editor's Note:** Using beef broth adds a deep rich flavor to the gravy.

Chicken Mozzarella

Jan Ellenbogen, Villa Ridge, Missouri

(PICTURED ON PAGE 62)

I like to make this Italian chicken for friends and family. It's delicious served with spaghetti, a tossed salad and garlic bread. Why not try it tonight?

  1/2 cup buttermilk baking mix
      2 tablespoons grated Parmesan cheese
  1/2 teaspoon Italian seasoning
  1/2 teaspoon paprika
  1/4 teaspoon pepper
      6 boneless skinless chicken breast halves
      1 cup spaghetti sauce
  3/4 cup shredded mozzarella cheese

Combine baking mix, Parmesan cheese, Italian seasoning, paprika and pepper; coat chicken. Place in a greased shallow baking dish. Bake, uncovered, at 400° for 10 minutes. Turn chicken and bake an additional 10 minutes. Pour sauce over chicken. Reduce heat to 350°; bake for 15-20 minutes or until juices run clear. Sprinkle with mozzarella cheese during the last few minutes of baking. **Yield:** 6 servings.

Key Lime Chicken Thighs

Idella Koen, Metolius, Oregon

(PICTURED ON PAGE 63)

I've been cooking since I was a girl and I like trying new recipes. Lime juice is a nice change of pace from the lemon juice used in many chicken dishes.

      8 chicken thighs (about 2 pounds), skin removed
      3 tablespoons butter *or* margarine
      2 to 3 tablespoons lime juice
    12 to 16 drops hot pepper sauce
      1 teaspoon brown sugar

1 teaspoon chicken bouillon granules
1/2 teaspoon *each* poultry seasoning and salt
1/2 teaspoon dried rosemary, crushed
1/4 to 1/2 teaspoon pepper
1/4 teaspoon paprika

Place chicken pieces in a greased 13-in. x 9-in. x 2-in. baking dish. Dot with butter; sprinkle with lime juice and hot pepper sauce. Combine remaining ingredients; sprinkle evenly over chicken. Bake, uncovered, at 425° for 30 minutes or until juices run clear. **Yield:** 4 servings.

German Chicken
Grace Nelson, Lakewood, Colorado

I came up with this chicken and cabbage dish on my own. But I owe it all to my two grandmothers, who taught me everything they know about cooking traditional German dishes.

1 broiler-fryer chicken (3-1/2 to 4 pounds), cut up
3/4 cup all-purpose flour
3 tablespoons butter *or* margarine
3 tablespoons cooking oil
3/4 teaspoon garlic powder, *divided*
1/2 teaspoon pepper, *divided*
1 large head green cabbage (3 pounds), coarsely chopped
1 large onion, chopped
1 can (29 ounces) sauerkraut, rinsed and drained
1 can (15 ounces) tomato sauce
1/3 cup packed brown sugar
1/4 cup cider vinegar

Coat chicken pieces with flour. In a large skillet, heat butter and oil; brown chicken on all sides. Place in a large Dutch oven or roaster; sprinkle with 1/4 teaspoon garlic powder and 1/8 teaspoon pepper. Top with half of the cabbage and onion. In a bowl, combine sauerkraut, tomato sauce, brown sugar, vinegar and remaining garlic powder and pepper. Pour half over the cabbage and onion. Repeat layers. Cover and bake at 350° for 1-1/2 hours or until chicken juices run clear and cabbage is tender. **Yield:** 4 servings.

Chicken Barbecued in Foil
Margaret Sharp, Ephrata, Pennsylvania

My family is happy when I serve barbecued chicken at unexpected times throughout the year. I'm glad to do it...the use of foil in this oven version means no mess!

3/4 cup chopped onion
1/2 cup ketchup
1/4 cup lemon juice
3 tablespoons butter *or* margarine
2 tablespoons Worcestershire sauce
1 tablespoon brown sugar
1 teaspoon dry mustard
1 teaspoon vinegar
1 broiler-fryer chicken (3-1/2 to 4 pounds), cut up and skin removed

Salt and pepper to taste
4 sheets heavy-duty aluminum foil (18 inches x 12 inches)

In a saucepan, combine the first eight ingredients; bring to a boil. Reduce heat; simmer, uncovered, for 15 minutes. Place 2 pieces of chicken in the center of each piece of foil; fold up edges to hold sauce. Sprinkle chicken with salt and pepper. Spoon sauce over chicken. Bring opposite long edges of foil together over the top and fold down several times. Fold the short ends toward the chicken and crimp tightly to prevent leaks. Place packets on a baking sheet. Bake at 350° for 1 hour. Carefully open packets and turn down foil. Broil chicken for 5 minutes or until browned. **Yield:** 4 servings.

Deluxe Baked Potatoes
Jenny Riegsecker, Delta, Ohio

Chicken, vegetables and cheese really liven up plain potatoes in this mouth-watering version. These splendid spuds are easy to assemble at the last minute.

2 baking potatoes (about 10 ounces *each*)
Cooking oil
1-1/2 cups cubed cooked chicken
1 package (10 ounces) frozen chopped broccoli, thawed and drained
1 jar (4-1/2 ounces) whole mushrooms, drained
3/4 teaspoon salt
1/4 teaspoon pepper
SAUCE:
1/2 cup chopped onion
2 tablespoons butter *or* margarine
2 tablespoons all-purpose flour
1/4 teaspoon salt
1/8 teaspoon pepper
1 cup milk
1-1/4 cups (5 ounces) shredded cheddar cheese, *divided*

Brush each potato with oil; prick with a fork. Bake at 400° for 60-70 minutes or until tender. Cool 10 minutes. Cut potatoes in half lengthwise. Scoop out pulp, leaving a 1/4-in. shell; set shells aside. Mash pulp. Add chicken, broccoli, mushrooms, salt and pepper; mix well. In a saucepan, saute onion in butter until tender. Add flour, salt and pepper; stir until smooth. Gradually add milk, stirring constantly. Bring to a boil; cook for 1 minute. Remove from the heat; stir in 1 cup cheese until melted. Add 1/3 cup sauce to potato mixture; toss to blend. Fill potato shells. Place in a greased 8-in. square baking dish. Pour remaining sauce over potatoes and sprinkle with remaining cheese. Bake at 400° for 20-25 minutes or until bubbly. **Yield:** 4 servings.

Cinnamon-Apricot Chicken Breasts

Margaret Botkin, Lilburn, Georgia
(PICTURED AT LEFT)

Whenever I offer this chicken to guests, they not only say they like it, they empty the plate. That's the best compliment a cook can ever receive!

- 2 cups water
- 1 cinnamon stick
- 6 tablespoons butter *or* margarine, *divided*
- 1 tablespoon sugar
- 1 teaspoon salt
- 1 cup uncooked long grain rice
- 6 boneless skinless chicken breast halves
- 1 small onion, finely chopped
- 1 garlic clove, minced
- 1-1/2 cups chicken broth
- 1 cup coarsely chopped dried apricots
- 1/3 cup fresh orange juice
- 2 tablespoons fresh lemon juice
- 1 teaspoon grated orange peel
- 1/2 teaspoon dried savory
- 3/4 cup coarsely chopped pecans

In a large saucepan, combine water, cinnamon stick, 2 tablespoons butter, sugar and salt; bring to a boil. Stir in rice. Reduce heat; cover and simmer until liquid is absorbed and rice is tender, about 20 minutes. Set aside. In a large skillet, cook chicken in remaining butter over medium-high heat until browned. Remove and set aside. In the same skillet, saute onion and garlic over medium-low heat until onion is tender. Stir in broth, apricots, juices, peel and savory; simmer for 5 minutes. Remove cinnamon stick from rice; stir in apricot mixture. Spoon into a greased 13-in. x 9-in. x 2-in. baking dish; top with chicken. Cover and bake at 350° for 20 minutes. Uncover; sprinkle with pecans and bake for 10 minutes or until juices run clear. **Yield:** 6 servings.

Harvest Stuffed Chicken

Jodi Cigel, Stevens Point, Wisconsin
(PICTURED AT LEFT)

This roasted chicken is easy enough to prepare every day, yet special enough for company. The corn bread and savory enhance the flavor of the homemade stuffing.

- 1 box (7-1/2 ounces) corn bread/muffin mix, prepared as directed and crumbled *or* 3 cups corn bread crumbs
- 3 cups unseasoned stuffing croutons
- 1/2 cup *each* chopped celery, fresh mushrooms and fully cooked ham
- 1/4 cup chopped sweet red pepper
- 1/4 cup chopped green onions
- 4 teaspoons chopped fresh savory *or* 1 teaspoon dried savory

---

MMM-MEATY MAINSTAYS. *Pictured at left, top to bottom: Harvest Stuffed Chicken, Peachy Chicken and Cinnamon-Apricot Chicken Breasts (all recipes on this page).*

- 3/4 teaspoon salt
- 1/2 teaspoon pepper
- 3 tablespoons cooking oil
- 1 to 1-1/2 cups chicken broth
- 1 roasting chicken (6 to 7 pounds)

In a large bowl, combine corn bread crumbs and croutons. In a large skillet, saute celery, mushrooms, ham, red pepper, onions, savory, salt and pepper in oil until vegetables are tender. Add to crumb mixture. Stir in enough broth to moisten. Stuff chicken. Place on a rack in a large roasting pan. Bake, uncovered, at 325° for 2-1/2 to 3 hours or until juices run clear. Or bake stuffing separately in a greased 2-qt. covered casserole at 350° for 45 minutes. **Yield:** 6 servings.

Peachy Chicken

Carol Ann McNeese, Albin, Indiana
(PICTURED AT LEFT)

I first tried this delicious dish at my sister's house and was delighted when she shared the recipe with me. Peaches give ordinary chicken a sweet taste and pretty golden color.

- 1 broiler-fryer chicken (3-1/2 to 4 pounds), cut up
- Salt and pepper to taste
- 1/4 cup molasses
- 3 tablespoons lemon juice
- 2 tablespoons butter *or* margarine, melted
- 2 tablespoons minced onion
- 3/4 teaspoon ground ginger
- 1 can (28 ounces) peach slices, drained

Place chicken in a greased 13-in. x 9-in. x 2-in. baking dish. Broil 6 minutes per side or until lightly browned. Season with salt and pepper. Combine molasses, lemon juice, butter, onion and ginger; pour over chicken. Bake, uncovered, at 375° for 30 minutes. Add peaches; baste chicken. Return to the oven for 10 minutes or until chicken juices run clear and peaches are heated through. **Yield:** 4 servings.

Berry Delicious Barbecue

Ena Quiggle, Goodhue, Minnesota

I met my wonderful husband while we were attending the same college here in Minnesota. I never thought I'd be a farmer's wife raising pigs and sheep, but I love country life!

- 12 chicken legs, skin removed
- 1 can (16 ounces) whole-berry cranberry sauce
- 1 can (10-3/4 ounces) condensed tomato soup, undiluted
- 1 envelope onion soup mix
- 2 tablespoons vinegar
- 1 tablespoon sugar
- 1/4 teaspoon garlic powder
- 1/4 teaspoon pepper

Place chicken in a greased 13-in. x 9-in. x 2-in. baking dish. Combine remaining ingredients; pour over chicken. Bake, uncovered, at 400° for 40-45 minutes or until juices run clear. **Yield:** 6-8 servings.

Hungarian Cabbage Bake
Ruth Kannenberg, Luverne, Minnesota

When we had a bumper crop of cabbage a few years back, I searched for new cabbage entrees. I was delighted to find this one…and happy when my family said they loved it.

    1/4 cup butter *or* margarine
      1 broiler-fryer chicken (3 to 3-1/2 pounds), cut up
      2 teaspoons paprika
      1 medium cabbage, cut into 1/2-inch slices
    3/4 teaspoon salt
    1/4 teaspoon pepper
      2 medium tart apples, sliced
      1 medium onion, chopped
      1 tablespoon caraway seed
      2 teaspoons grated lemon peel
      1 teaspoon sugar
      1 cup (4 ounces) shredded Swiss cheese, optional

In a large skillet, heat butter over medium heat. Sprinkle chicken with paprika; brown on all sides. Reduce heat; cover and simmer for 20 minutes. Meanwhile, place cabbage in a greased 13-in. x 9-in. x 2-in. baking dish. Sprinkle with salt and pepper. Cover tightly. Bake at 375° for 20 minutes. Arrange apples and onion over cabbage. Sprinkle with caraway, lemon peel and sugar. Top with chicken pieces. Cover; bake for 30 minutes or until chicken juices run clear and cabbage is tender. Uncover; sprinkle with cheese if desired. Return to the oven for 5 minutes or until cheese melts. **Yield:** 4 servings.

Chicken Pizzas
Dorothy Near, Cowansville, Quebec

Students in a high school course were asked to prepare a well-balanced meal for their families. My grandson created this pizza. I know you'll like it as much as we do!

CRUST:
      1 package (1/4 ounce) active dry yeast
      1 cup warm water (110° to 115°)
    2-3/4 to 3 cups all-purpose flour
      1 tablespoon vegetable oil
      1 tablespoon sugar
    1/2 teaspoon salt
TOPPING:
      1 can (10-3/4 ounces) condensed cream of
         mushroom soup, undiluted
      1 teaspoon paprika
      1 teaspoon dried oregano
    1/2 teaspoon garlic powder
    1/2 teaspoon salt
    1/4 teaspoon pepper
      1 medium green pepper, chopped
      1 small onion, chopped
    1/2 pound fresh mushrooms, sliced
      1 cup diced cooked chicken
    1-1/2 cups (6 ounces) shredded cheddar cheese
    2-1/2 cups (10 ounces) shredded mozzarella cheese

In a large mixing bowl, dissolve yeast in water. Add 1-1/2 cups flour, oil, sugar and salt; beat until smooth.

Add enough remaining flour to form a soft dough. Turn onto a floured board; knead until smooth and elastic, about 6-8 minutes. Place in a greased bowl, turning once to grease top. Cover and let rise in a warm place until doubled, about 1 hour. Punch dough down. Divide in half and roll each half into a 13-in. circle. Place each piece on a lightly greased 12- to 13-in. pizza pan. Combine soup, paprika, oregano, garlic powder, salt and pepper; spread over each pizza. Layer with green pepper, onion, mushrooms and chicken. Combine cheeses; sprinkle over pizzas. Bake at 425° for 20-25 minutes or until crust is browned and cheese is melted. **Yield:** 12-16 servings (2 pizzas).

> **BEAUTIFUL BIRD.** Give chicken a pleasant golden-brown color by sprinkling with paprika before baking.

Saucy Muffin Cups
Karen Lehman, Aberdeen, Idaho

I don't have a lot of time on my hands. But after busy days on our dairy farm, everyone expects a good hearty supper. So I came up with this simple savory dish.

      1 loaf (1 pound) frozen bread dough, thawed *or*
         12 dinner roll dough portions
      2 cups diced cooked chicken
      1 can (10-3/4 ounces) condensed cream of
         mushroom soup, undiluted
    1/4 cup sliced ripe olives, drained
    1/2 cup sliced frozen carrots, thawed
      2 tablespoons minced fresh parsley
      1 teaspoon chicken bouillon granules
    1/4 teaspoon garlic powder
Dash pepper
    1/2 cup shredded sharp cheddar cheese

If using bread dough, punch down and divide into 12 pieces. Flatten each piece or roll into a 6-in. circle. Press circles into the bottom and up the sides of greased muffin cups. In a saucepan, combine remaining ingredients except cheese; cook and stir for 5 minutes or until heated through. Spoon into bread cups; sprinkle with cheese. Bake, uncovered, at 350° for 25-30 minutes or until browned. **Yield:** 6 servings.

Crowd-Pleasing Rice Bake
Nadine Proffitt, Mechanicsville, Virginia

Although I work full-time outside of the home, one of my favorite things to do when I have time is cook. This dish is perfect to take along to potlucks.

      9 cups chicken broth
      3 packages (about 2-1/2 ounces *each*) dry
         chicken noodle soup mix
      2 cups uncooked long grain rice
      1 pound bulk pork sausage
    1-1/2 cups sliced celery
      2 large onions, chopped
      2 medium green peppers, chopped

        1 can (10-3/4 ounces) condensed cream of
          mushroom soup, undiluted
        6 cups cubed cooked chicken
      1/2 cup slivered almonds, toasted

In a large saucepan, bring broth to a boil. Stir in soup mixes; simmer for 10 minutes. Add rice; simmer for 15 minutes. Remove from the heat and set aside. In a large skillet over medium heat, brown and crumble sausage until no longer pink. Remove with a slotted spoon and set aside. Discard all but 1 tablespoon drippings. Saute celery, onions and peppers in drippings until tender. Stir in sausage, mushroom soup, chicken and rice mixture until well mixed. Pour into two greased 2-1/2-qt. baking dishes. Cover and bake at 350° for 30 minutes or until rice is tender. Sprinkle with almonds. **Yield:** 18 servings.

Creamy Chicken and Vegetables
Joyce Bromeland, Rake, Iowa

I own and operate a restaurant in our town. My customers love meat and potatoes, but occasionally I'll offer a tasty new menu item, like this flavorful chicken.

        6 boneless skinless chicken breast halves
        3 tablespoons butter *or* margarine, *divided*
        1 *each* medium green pepper, sweet red pepper
          and onion, julienned
      1/2 pound fresh mushrooms, sliced
        1 package (10 ounces) frozen cut broccoli,
          thawed and drained
        1 can (10-3/4 ounces) condensed cream of
          broccoli soup, undiluted
        1 cup (8 ounces) sour cream
        1 teaspoon salt
      1/2 teaspoon pepper
      1/2 teaspoon dried rosemary, crushed

In a skillet over medium heat, brown chicken in 2 tablespoons butter. Set aside; discard drippings. In the same skillet, saute peppers and onion in remaining butter for 5 minutes or until crisp-tender. Add mushrooms and broccoli; cook for 3-5 minutes or until heated through. Add soup, sour cream, salt, pepper and rosemary; stir to mix. Spread half into a greased 13-in. x 9-in. x 2-in. baking dish. Add chicken; top with remaining vegetable mixture. Cover and bake at 350° for 30 minutes. Uncover and bake 10 minutes more or until bubbly and chicken juices run clear. **Yield:** 6 servings.

Zesty Corn Bread with Creamed Chicken
Shirley Heston, Lancaster, Ohio

I first made this creamed chicken many years ago when I was taking a home economics class. It's great to serve at a brunch, and even children find it hard to resist!

        1 package (8-1/2 ounces) corn bread/muffin mix
        3 tablespoons finely chopped onion, *divided*
        1 teaspoon paprika
        1 chicken bouillon cube

      1/2 cup boiling water
        1 jar (4-1/2 ounces) sliced mushrooms, drained
      1/4 cup chopped green pepper
        3 tablespoons butter *or* margarine
        3 tablespoons all-purpose flour
      1/2 teaspoon salt
      1/4 teaspoon pepper
Dash hot pepper sauce
        1 can (12 ounces) evaporated milk
        2 cups cubed cooked chicken
        2 tablespoons chopped pimientos

Prepare corn bread mix according to package directions, adding 2 tablespoons onion and the paprika. Spoon into a well-greased 4- to 5-cup ring mold. Bake at 400° for 15 minutes or until a toothpick inserted near the center comes out clean. Let stand for 5 minutes. Turn out onto a serving platter. Meanwhile, dissolve bouillon in water; set aside. In a medium saucepan, saute mushrooms, green pepper and remaining onion in butter until tender. Stir in flour, salt, pepper and hot pepper sauce until smooth. Add milk and prepared bouillon; cook over medium heat for 2 minutes or until thickened and bubbly, stirring constantly. Cook for 2-3 minutes. Add chicken and pimientos; heat through. Spoon over corn bread. **Yield:** 4-6 servings.

Herbed Chicken
Diane Cigel, Stevens Point, Wisconsin

This is such a versatile dish because it can be made in the oven or microwave...so time is never a factor. People always comment on the chicken's wonderful subtle herb flavor.

✓ **This tasty dish uses less sugar, salt and fat. Recipe includes** *Diabetic Exchanges.*

      3/4 to 1 cup water
        1 tablespoon chicken bouillon granules
      1/2 teaspoon dried thyme
      1/2 teaspoon dried rosemary, crushed
        2 bay leaves
        1 broiler-fryer chicken (3-1/2 to 4 pounds)
        1 pound new potatoes, halved
        2 medium onions, cut into 1/2-inch pieces
        2 carrots, cut into 1/2-inch pieces

Combine 1 cup water, bouillon, thyme, rosemary and bay leaves; pour into a roasting pan. Add chicken; arrange potatoes, onions and carrots around it. Cover and bake at 350° for 50 minutes. Uncover; bake for 20-30 minutes or until vegetables are tender and chicken juices run clear. Remove the bay leaves before serving. **Microwave Directions:** In a 3-qt. microwave-safe baking dish, combine 3/4 cup water, bouillon, thyme, rosemary and bay leaves. Place chicken, breast side down, in dish. Cover and cook on high for 10 minutes. Turn chicken over and arrange vegetables around it. Cover and cook at 50% power for 30-40 minutes or until vegetables are tender and chicken juices run clear. Remove bay leaves. This recipe was tested in a 700-watt microwave. **Yield:** 4 servings. **Diabetic Exchanges:** One serving (prepared with low-sodium bouillon) equals 2-1/2 lean meat, 1 starch, 1 vegetable; also, 213 calories, 89 mg sodium, 62 mg cholesterol, 20 gm carbohydrate, 24 gm protein, 4 gm fat.

Comforting Casseroles

Cooks across the country count on the convenience of fast and flavorful one-dish meals. Every down-home helping pleases any hungry clan!

Lemon-Curry Chicken Casserole
Sue Yaeger, Brookings, South Dakota
(PICTURED AT LEFT)

Asparagus and almonds add a flavorful twist to an ordinary chicken dish. I've made this countless times for company and am usually asked for the recipe.

2 packages (12 ounces *each*) frozen cut
   asparagus, thawed and drained
4 boneless skinless chicken breast halves, cut
   into 1/2-inch strips
Salt and pepper to taste
3 tablespoons butter *or* margarine
1 can (10-3/4 ounces) condensed cream of
   chicken soup, undiluted
1/2 cup mayonnaise
1/4 cup lemon juice
1 teaspoon curry powder
1/4 teaspoon ground ginger
1/8 teaspoon pepper
1/2 cup sliced almonds, toasted

Place asparagus in a greased 11-in. x 7-in. x 2-in. baking dish; set aside. Sprinkle chicken with salt and pepper. In a large skillet, saute chicken in butter for 10-14 minutes or until juices run clear. Place over asparagus. Combine soup, mayonnaise, lemon juice, curry powder, ginger and pepper; spoon over chicken. Bake, uncovered, at 350° for 35 minutes. Sprinkle with almonds and return to the oven for 5 minutes. **Yield:** 6 servings.

Summer Squash Enchiladas
DeAnna Steed, Ignacio, Colorado

I especially like to serve these enchiladas when squash is readily available in our garden. Everyone who tries them likes the fresh saucy flavor.

3/4 cup chopped onion
2 garlic cloves, minced
1 tablespoon cooking oil
3 cups chopped yellow squash
2 cups cubed cooked chicken
1 can (4 ounces) chopped green chilies
2 tablespoons butter *or* margarine
2 tablespoons all-purpose flour
2 teaspoons chili powder
1/4 teaspoon salt
1/8 teaspoon pepper

SECONDS, PLEASE! *Pictured at left, top to bottom: Lemon-Curry Chicken Casserole and Savory-Crust Chicken Pie (both recipes on this page).*

1-1/4 cups milk
10 flour tortillas (6 to 8 inches)
1-1/2 cups (6 ounces) shredded Monterey Jack
   cheese, *divided*
1 cup chopped fresh tomatoes
Sour cream

In a skillet, saute onion and garlic in oil until tender. Add squash and saute until tender. Add chicken and chilies; heat through. In a saucepan, melt butter. Add flour, chili powder, salt and pepper; stir to form a smooth paste. Gradually add milk, stirring constantly. Cook until sauce comes to a boil; cook an additional minute until thickened. Add 1/3 cup sauce to chicken mixture; mix well. Place 1/3 to 1/2 cup chicken mixture down the center of each tortilla; top with 1 tablespoon cheese. Roll up and place seam side down in a greased 13-in. x 9-in. x 2-in. baking dish. Spread remaining sauce on top. Cover and bake at 400° for 25 minutes. Uncover; sprinkle with tomatoes and remaining cheese. Return to the oven for 5 minutes. Serve with sour cream. **Yield:** 4-6 servings.

Savory-Crust Chicken Pie
Michelle Bentley, Niceville, Florida
(PICTURED AT LEFT)

Everyone will love the hearty combination of vegetables, chicken and sauce in this unique version of chicken potpie. And the tasty homemade crust is so simple to prepare.

CRUST:
1 cup (8 ounces) sour cream
1/2 cup butter *or* margarine, softened
1 egg
1 cup all-purpose flour
1 teaspoon baking powder
1 teaspoon salt
1 teaspoon dried sage
FILLING:
1/2 cup *each* chopped carrots, green pepper,
   sweet red pepper and onion
1/2 cup sliced fresh mushrooms
2 tablespoons butter *or* margarine
2 cups cubed cooked chicken
1 can (10-3/4 ounces) condensed cream of
   chicken soup, undiluted
1/2 cup shredded cheddar cheese

In a mixing bowl, beat sour cream, butter and egg. Add flour, baking powder, salt and sage; mix well (mixture will be sticky). Spread into the bottom and up the sides of an ungreased 10-in. pie plate. For filling, saute vegetables in butter over medium heat until crisp-tender. Add chicken and soup; mix well. Spoon into the crust. Sprinkle with cheese. Bake at 400° for 30-35 minutes or until lightly browned. Let stand for 10 minutes. Spoon out individual servings. **Yield:** 6-8 servings.

Lasagna Deluxe
Betty Rutherford, St. George, Utah

You don't need to precook the noodles in this variation of an Italian classic, so it's perfect for the family during the week and for guests on the weekend.

- 1 cup cottage cheese
- 1 package (3 ounces) cream cheese, softened
- 1 can (10-3/4 ounces) condensed cream of mushroom soup, undiluted
- 1-1/2 cups chopped fresh broccoli
- 1/2 cup chopped celery
- 1/3 cup chopped onion
- 1/4 cup milk
- 1/2 teaspoon poultry seasoning
- 6 uncooked lasagna noodles
- 1-1/2 cups cubed cooked chicken
- 1/2 cup shredded Monterey Jack cheese
- 2/3 cup boiling water

In a small bowl, combine cottage cheese and cream cheese; set aside. In another bowl, combine the next six ingredients; set aside. Place two lasagna noodles in a greased 11-in. x 7-in. x 2-in. baking dish. Top with half the cottage cheese mixture and a third of the broccoli mixture. Repeat layers of noodles, cheese and broccoli. Top with two noodles, chicken and remaining broccoli mixture. Sprinkle with Monterey Jack cheese. Pour boiling water around edges of dish. Cover tightly and bake at 350° for 60-65 minutes. Leave covered and let stand for 10 minutes before serving. **Yield:** 6 servings.

Chicken and Spinach Supper
Donna Nizolek, Chester, New York

This recipe appeared in a school cookbook I put together while working as a teacher's aide. Everyone will think you fussed all day...but it just takes minutes to put together.

✓ This tasty dish uses less sugar, salt and fat. Recipe includes *Diabetic Exchanges*.

- 4 packages (10 ounces *each*) frozen chopped spinach, thawed and well drained
- 1/4 teaspoon ground nutmeg
- 1 teaspoon salt, *divided*, optional
- 4 cups diced cooked chicken
- 1/4 cup butter *or* margarine
- 1/4 cup all-purpose flour
- 1/4 teaspoon pepper
- 1/8 teaspoon paprika
- 2 cups chicken broth
- 1 tablespoon lemon juice
- 1/2 teaspoon dried rosemary, crushed

TOPPING:
- 1 tablespoon butter *or* margarine, melted
- 1/2 cup bread crumbs
- 1/3 cup grated Parmesan cheese

Mix spinach, nutmeg and 1/2 teaspoon salt if desired. Pat in the bottom of a greased 13-in. x 9-in. x 2-in. baking dish. Top with chicken. Melt butter in a saucepan. Add flour, pepper, paprika and remaining salt if desired;

stir to form a smooth paste. Gradually add broth, lemon juice and rosemary, stirring constantly. Bring to a boil; cook an additional minute until thickened. Pour over chicken. Combine topping ingredients; sprinkle over casserole. Bake, uncovered, at 350° for 40-45 minutes or until bubbly. **Yield:** 8 servings. **Diabetic Exchanges:** One serving (prepared with margarine and low-sodium broth and without added salt) equals 4 lean meat, 1 vegetable, 1/2 starch; also, 298 calories, 307 mg sodium, 73 mg cholesterol, 14 gm carbohydrate, 31 gm protein, 12 gm fat.

Chicken 'n' Noodles for Two
Verna Keinath, Millington, Michigan

I discovered this recipe quite a few years ago. It's a fast and flavorful supper that's just the right size for us "empty-nesters". But it can be easily doubled for guests.

- 1/2 cup cottage cheese
- 1/4 cup mayonnaise *or* salad dressing
- 1/4 cup chopped onion
- 2 tablespoons chopped green pepper
- 1 tablespoon chopped pimientos
- 1 teaspoon Dijon mustard
- 1/2 teaspoon Worcestershire sauce
- 1/2 teaspoon chopped fresh chives
- 2 drops hot pepper sauce
- 1 cup cubed cooked chicken
- 1 cup cooked dumpling egg noodles
- 1/2 cup frozen peas, thawed
- 1/8 teaspoon ground paprika

In a bowl, combine first nine ingredients. Toss with chicken, noodles and peas. Spoon into a greased 1-qt. casserole; sprinkle with paprika. Bake, uncovered, at 350° for 25-30 minutes or until bubbly. **Yield:** 2 servings.

Chicken Almondine
Alice Ganskop, Flaxton, North Dakota

My husband and I keep busy on our farm. So I appreciate meals like this that are simple yet satisfying.

- 1 cup sliced celery
- 1 cup chopped green pepper
- 1/2 cup chopped onion
- 1 tablespoon butter *or* margarine
- 3 cups cubed cooked chicken
- 2 cups cooked rice
- 1 cup chicken broth
- 1 package (10 ounces) frozen peas, thawed
- 1 jar (2 ounces) diced pimientos, drained
- 1/2 teaspoon salt
- 1/4 teaspoon pepper
- 2 cans (10-3/4 ounces *each*) condensed cream of chicken soup, undiluted
- 3/4 cup mayonnaise

TOPPING:
- 7 ounces sage and onion stuffing
- 2/3 cup sliced almonds
- 3/4 cup butter *or* margarine, melted

In a large skillet, saute celery, green pepper and onion in butter until tender; remove from the heat. Add chicken, rice, broth, peas, pimientos, salt and pepper; mix well. Spoon into a greased 13-in. x 9-in. x 2-in. baking dish. Combine soup and mayonnaise; spread over chicken mixture. For topping, combine stuffing and almonds; sprinkle over casserole. Drizzle with butter. Cover and bake at 350° for 30 minutes. Uncover and bake 15 minutes longer or until bubbly. **Yield:** 6-8 servings.

Cordon Bleu Casserole
Colleen Baker, Wonewoc, Wisconsin

With its ease of preparation, I'm sure this casserole will become one of your favorite one-dish meals. The rich creamy sauce is sure to please your family!

6 slices whole wheat bread
6 chicken breast halves, cooked and sliced
1 package (8 ounces) cream cheese, thinly sliced
1/2 pound sliced fully cooked ham
1-1/2 cups (6 ounces) shredded Swiss cheese, *divided*
2 packages (10 ounces *each*) frozen broccoli spears, thawed and drained
2 cans (10-3/4 ounces *each*) condensed cream of chicken soup, undiluted
1/4 teaspoon pepper

Place bread in the bottom of a greased 13-in. x 9-in. x 2-in. baking dish. Layer chicken, cream cheese slices and ham over bread. Sprinkle with 1 cup Swiss cheese. Top with broccoli. Combine soup and pepper; spoon over broccoli. Sprinkle with remaining Swiss cheese. Bake, uncovered, at 350° for 50-55 minutes or until bubbly. **Yield:** 8-10 servings.

Texas Pie
Dianne Slama, Lincoln, Nebraska

I'll prepare this recipe when my family has a taste for Southwestern cooking. It's a good way to use leftover chicken and nice when dinner has to be done in a hurry.

1/4 cup chopped onion
2 tablespoons butter *or* margarine
1-1/2 cups cubed cooked chicken
1 can (4 ounces) chopped green chilies, drained
1 jar (4-1/2 ounces) sliced mushrooms, drained
1 can (10-3/4 ounces) condensed cream of chicken soup, undiluted
1/2 cup sour cream
1/4 teaspoon hot pepper sauce
1 cup (4 ounces) shredded mozzarella cheese
1 pastry shell (9 inches), baked
1/2 cup shredded cheddar cheese

In a saucepan, saute onion in butter until tender. Stir in chicken, chilies and mushrooms. In a small bowl, combine soup, sour cream and hot pepper sauce; add to pan. Cook and stir for 5 minutes. Sprinkle mozzarella cheese in the bottom of pie shell; add chicken mixture.

Sprinkle with cheddar cheese. Bake at 350° for 25-30 minutes or until filling is bubbly and cheese is melted. **Yield:** 6-8 servings.

Corny Bread Bake
Janice France, Louisville, Kentucky

My family used to turn up their noses at casseroles, but then I put this on the table. Everyone enjoyed the slightly spicy filling...and even asked when I could make it again!

2 cups cubed cooked chicken
1-1/2 cups (6 ounces) shredded Monterey Jack cheese
1 can (11 ounces) Mexican-style corn, drained
1 can (4 ounces) chopped green chilies, drained
1 cup buttermilk baking mix
3 eggs, *separated*
1 cup milk
1/2 teaspoon salt

Combine chicken, cheese, corn and chilies; place in a greased shallow 2-1/2-qt. baking dish. In a mixing bowl, beat baking mix, egg yolks, milk and salt until smooth. In another mixing bowl, beat egg whites until stiff peaks form; fold into yolk mixture. Pour over chicken mixture. Bake, uncovered, at 350° for 40-45 minutes or until browned and a knife inserted near the center comes out clean. **Yield:** 4-6 servings.

Chicken Livers Royale
Ann Shaw, Vermilion, Ohio

I'm a retired home economics teacher, but my son does most of the cooking around here. As a matter of fact, he created this delightful dish, which is truly "fit for a king"!

1/2 cup seasoned croutons
1 pound chicken livers, cut into bite-size pieces
2 tablespoons olive *or* vegetable oil, *divided*
1 cup sliced fresh mushrooms
1/2 cup chopped onion
1 garlic clove, minced
16 pitted ripe olives, halved, optional
4 bacon strips, cooked and crumbled
1/2 cup spaghetti sauce
4 eggs
1 cup (4 ounces) shredded mozzarella cheese
1/4 cup chopped fresh parsley

Coat four individual 10-oz. baking dishes with nonstick cooking spray. Divide croutons among dishes; set aside. In a large skillet, saute chicken livers in 1 tablespoon oil for about 8 minutes or until outsides are lightly browned and centers are still slightly pink. Remove with a slotted spoon and place over croutons. Discard drippings; add remaining oil to skillet. Saute mushrooms, onion, garlic and olives if desired until tender. Remove with a slotted spoon and place over chicken livers. Sprinkle with bacon; top with spaghetti sauce. Break an egg into each dish. Bake, uncovered, at 325° for 25-30 minutes or until eggs reach desired doneness. Sprinkle with parsley. Serve immediately. **Yield:** 4 servings.

Cheddar Chicken Mostaccioli

Mrs. Troy Hawk, Sheridan, Missouri
(PICTURED AT LEFT)

While growing up, I enjoyed cooking for the whole family. So it's no surprise that I'm now a dietician. This casserole was popular in a cafeteria where I once worked.

- 1/2 cup chopped onion
- 1/2 cup chopped celery
- 1 tablespoon butter *or* margarine
- 1 can (10-3/4 ounces) condensed cream of mushroom soup, undiluted
- 1 can (10-3/4 ounces) condensed cream of chicken soup, undiluted
- 1/2 cup milk
- 1 can (4 ounces) mushroom stems and pieces, drained
- 1 jar (2 ounces) diced pimientos, drained
- 1/4 cup chopped stuffed olives
- 1 tablespoon Worcestershire sauce
- 1-1/4 teaspoons garlic salt
- 1/2 teaspoon *each* dried basil, oregano and pepper
- 4 cups diced cooked chicken
- 3 cups mostaccioli, cooked and drained
- 1-1/4 cups (5 ounces) shredded cheddar cheese, *divided*
- 1 cup (4 ounces) shredded Swiss cheese

In a saucepan, saute onion and celery in butter until tender. Add soups, milk, mushrooms, pimientos, olives, Worcestershire sauce and seasonings; mix well. Add chicken, mostaccioli, 3/4 cup cheddar cheese and the Swiss cheese; toss to mix. Pour into a greased 13-in. x 9-in. x 2-in. baking dish. Cover and bake at 350° for 40 minutes. Uncover; sprinkle with remaining cheddar and return to the oven for 15 minutes. **Yield:** 6-8 servings.

Party Casserole

Becky MacIntyre, Troy, Michigan
(PICTURED AT LEFT)

I've been making this vegetable dish for years and recently added the chicken to make it a one-pan meal. It never fails to get raves from men and women alike!

- 6 boneless skinless chicken breast halves
- 1 cup water
- 2 cups sliced zucchini (1/4 inch thick)
- 1 package (14 ounces) frozen tiny whole carrots *or* 3 cups fresh baby carrots
- 5 tablespoons butter *or* margarine, *divided*
- 2 tablespoons all-purpose flour
- 1-1/2 cups half-and-half cream *or* milk
- 2 teaspoons chicken bouillon granules
- 1/2 teaspoon prepared mustard
- 1/2 teaspoon dill weed, *divided*

POTLUCK POSSIBILITIES. *Pictured at left, top to bottom: Cheddar Chicken Mostaccioli and Party Casserole (both recipes on this page).*

- 1/8 teaspoon pepper
- Dash nutmeg
- 1 can (14-1/2 ounces) small whole onions, drained
- 1-1/2 cups soft bread crumbs
- 3/4 cup shredded cheddar cheese
- 1/2 cup coarsely chopped walnuts

In a large skillet, bring chicken and water to a boil. Reduce heat and simmer, uncovered, for 3 minutes. Turn chicken and simmer 3 minutes longer (chicken will not be completely cooked). Remove chicken from cooking liquid and place down the center of an ungreased 13-in. x 9-in. x 2-in. baking dish; set aside. Cook zucchini and carrots in cooking liquid for 5 minutes or until zucchini just begins to soften; drain and set aside. In a large saucepan, melt 2 tablespoons butter; stir in flour and cook for 1 minute. Stir in cream until smooth. Add bouillon, mustard, 1/4 teaspoon dill, pepper and nutmeg. Bring to a boil, stirring constantly; cook for 2 minutes. Remove from the heat. Spoon 1/2 cup sauce over chicken. Add zucchini, carrots and onions to remaining sauce. Spoon along sides of baking dish. Melt remaining butter; toss with bread crumbs, cheese, walnuts and remaining dill. Spoon over chicken and vegetables. Bake, uncovered, at 375° for 30-35 minutes or until topping is browned and sauce is bubbly. **Yield:** 6 servings.

Swiss Chicken Bake

Doris Cohn, Denville, New Jersey

I try to keep the ingredients for this creamy casserole on hand for last-minute meals. Whenever I serve this at family dinners and potlucks, it's well-received.

- 1 box (7 ounces) thin spaghetti, cooked and drained
- 1 package (10 ounces) frozen chopped spinach, thawed and well drained
- 1/2 cup half-and-half cream
- 1/3 cup Parmesan cheese, *divided*
- 1/2 teaspoon salt
- 1/4 teaspoon pepper
- 1/8 to 1/4 teaspoon ground nutmeg
- 2 cups diced cooked chicken
- 1 cup (4 ounces) shredded Swiss cheese
- 1/2 cup sliced fresh mushrooms
- 2 bacon strips, cooked and crumbled
- 4 eggs, lightly beaten
- 1 cup ricotta cheese
- 1/4 cup chopped onion
- 1 garlic clove, minced

Combine spaghetti, spinach, cream, 4 tablespoons Parmesan cheese, salt, pepper and nutmeg. Place in the bottom of a greased 9-in. square baking dish. Top with chicken, Swiss cheese, mushrooms and bacon. In a bowl, combine eggs, ricotta, onion and garlic; spread over chicken. Sprinkle with remaining Parmesan. Bake, uncovered, at 350° for 30-35 minutes or until bubbly. **Yield:** 4-6 servings.

Chicken and Dressing Dish
Anne Smith, Taylors, South Carolina

I've always enjoyed trying new recipes, and now that our children are grown, I have more time to do just that!

✓ This tasty dish uses less sugar, salt and fat. Recipe includes *Diabetic Exchanges*.

      1 cup chopped onion
      1 cup chopped celery
  1/4 cup butter *or* margarine
      2 cups chicken broth
1-1/2 teaspoons dried thyme
      1 teaspoon poultry seasoning
  1/2 teaspoon salt
  1/2 teaspoon pepper
  1/4 teaspoon ground nutmeg
      2 eggs, lightly beaten *or* egg substitute
          equivalent
      1 bag (12 ounces) unseasoned stuffing croutons
  1/4 cup chopped fresh parsley
      3 cups cubed cooked chicken
      1 can (10-3/4 ounces) condensed cream of
          chicken *or* mushroom soup, undiluted
  1/3 cup water

In a large saucepan, saute onion and celery in butter until tender; remove from the heat. Add broth, thyme, poultry seasoning, salt, pepper, nutmeg and eggs; mix well. Add bread cubes and parsley; toss to mix. Transfer to a greased 13-in. x 9-in. x 2-in. baking dish. Top with chicken. Combine soup and water; spoon over chicken. Let stand for 10 minutes. Cover and bake at 350° for 50 minutes. Uncover and bake an additional 5-10 minutes or until bubbly. **Yield:** 8 servings. **Diabetic Exchanges:** One serving (prepared with margarine, low-sodium broth, egg substitute and reduced-fat soup and without added salt) equals 2-1/2 starch, 2 lean meat, 1-1/2 fat, 1 vegetable; also, 390 calories, 572 mg sodium, 48 mg cholesterol, 41 gm carbohydrate, 26 gm protein, 13 gm fat.

Speedy Scalloped Potatoes
Marcille Meyer, Battle Creek, Nebraska

This recipe calls for boxed potatoes—so there's no peeling and slicing! And with leftover cooked chicken, it's a simple way to make a hearty one-dish dinner.

      1 box (5 ounces) scalloped potatoes with creamy
          cheese sauce
2-1/2 cups hot water
      1 can (10-3/4 ounces) condensed cream of
          chicken soup, undiluted
  1/2 teaspoon poultry seasoning
      2 cups cubed cooked chicken
      1 cup shredded carrots
  1/2 cup sliced celery
  1/4 cup chopped onion

In a bowl, combine sauce mix packet from potatoes with the water, soup and poultry seasoning; stir until well blended. Add potatoes and remaining ingredients; mix well. Pour into a greased 2-1/2-qt. baking dish. Bake, un-

covered, at 350° for 50-60 minutes or until potatoes are tender and top is golden. **Yield:** 4-6 servings.

Broccoli-Cheese Strata
Margery Moore, Richfield Springs, New York

On our dairy farm, chores often delay dinner. That's when this strata comes in handy. I'll prepare it beforehand and pop it in the oven for a quick and easy meal.

    12 slices buttered bread
2-1/4 cups (10 ounces) shredded cheddar cheese,
          divided
      1 package (10 ounces) frozen chopped broccoli,
          thawed and drained
      2 cups diced cooked chicken
      6 eggs
      3 cups milk
      2 tablespoons minced onion
  3/4 teaspoon salt
  1/2 teaspoon dry mustard
  1/4 teaspoon pepper

Using a doughnut cutter, cut 12 rings and holes from bread; set aside. Tear bread scraps and place in the bottom of a greased 13-in. x 9-in. x 2-in. baking dish. Sprinkle with 2 cups cheese, broccoli and chicken. Arrange rings and holes, with buttered sides up, on top. Beat eggs, milk, onion, salt, mustard and pepper; pour over casserole. Cover and refrigerate 8 hours or overnight. Remove from the refrigerator 30 minutes before baking. Bake, uncovered, at 325° for 55-60 minutes. Sprinkle with remaining cheese; return to the oven for 5 minutes until a knife inserted near the center comes out clean. Let stand for 5-10 minutes before cutting. **Yield:** 6-8 servings.

Cheesy Chicken and Rice
Rebekah Thurlow, New Wilmington, Pennsylvania

When autumn winds start to blow here in the Northeast, I keep this recipe close at hand. There are never any leftovers when I serve this to my family—much to their disappointment!

      3 cups cooked long grain rice
      1 package (10 ounces) frozen chopped broccoli,
          thawed and drained
      8 ounces fresh mushrooms, sliced
      2 tablespoons butter *or* margarine
      2 cups diced cooked chicken
  1/2 cup chopped green onions
      4 eggs
      1 cup milk
  1/2 teaspoon salt
  1/2 teaspoon pepper
      2 cups (8 ounces) shredded cheddar cheese,
          divided
      1 can (10-3/4 ounces) condensed cream of
          chicken soup, undiluted

Combine rice and broccoli; spoon into a greased 12-in. x 8-in. x 2-in. baking dish. In a large skillet, saute mushrooms in butter until tender. Remove from the heat. Add chicken and green onions; spoon over rice mixture. Beat eggs, milk, salt and pepper; pour over all. Sprinkle with 1 cup cheese. Spread soup over top. Bake, uncovered, at 350° for 30 minutes. Sprinkle with remaining cheese and bake 15 minutes longer. **Yield:** 6 servings.

Chicken-Mushroom Deluxe
Jean Voermans, Whitefish, Montana

My family could eat noodle dishes at every meal. For a change of pace from traditional spaghetti, I like this creamy casserole packed with chicken and mushrooms.

1-1/2 cups sliced fresh mushrooms
1/2 cup chopped onion
1/2 cup chopped green pepper
2 tablespoons butter *or* margarine
1 can (10-3/4 ounces) condensed cream of chicken soup, undiluted
1/2 cup milk
1/4 cup chopped pimientos
3/4 teaspoon dried basil
1 package (8 ounces) rotini pasta, cooked and drained
2 cups cottage cheese
1-1/2 cups (6 ounces) shredded cheddar cheese
1/2 cup grated Parmesan cheese, *divided*
3 cups cubed cooked chicken

In a skillet, saute mushrooms, onion and green pepper in butter until tender. Add soup, milk, pimientos and basil; mix well and heat through. Place pasta in the bottom of a greased 13-in. x 9-in. x 2-in. baking dish. Combine cottage cheese, cheddar and 1/4 cup Parmesan; spread over pasta. Top with chicken. Pour sauce over chicken. Sprinkle with remaining Parmesan. Cover and bake at 350° for 50-55 minutes or until bubbly. **Yield:** 6-8 servings.

Chicken Divan
Karren Raschein, Prairie du Sac, Wisconsin

Like all farm wives, I'm always on the go, so I often reach for this easy yet elegant recipe. What a great way to combine two great foods—chicken and broccoli!

✓ This tasty dish uses less sugar, salt and fat. Recipe includes *Diabetic Exchanges*.

1 package (10 ounces) frozen broccoli spears, thawed and drained
3 chicken breast halves, cooked and sliced
1 can (10-3/4 ounces) condensed cream of broccoli soup, undiluted
1/2 cup mayonnaise
1 teaspoon lemon juice
1 teaspoon butter *or* margarine, melted
1/4 cup soft bread crumbs
1/4 cup shredded Swiss cheese

Place broccoli spears in a greased 8-in. square baking dish. Top with chicken. Combine soup, mayonnaise and lemon juice; spread over chicken. Toss butter and bread crumbs; add cheese. Sprinkle over sauce. Bake, uncov-

ered, at 350° for 30-35 minutes or until bubbly. **Yield:** 4 servings. **Diabetic Exchanges:** One serving (prepared with light mayonnaise, margarine and low-fat cheese) equals 3 lean meat, 1 vegetable 1 starch; also, 311 calories, 510 mg sodium, 65 mg cholesterol, 15 gm carbohydrate, 25 gm protein, 13 gm fat.

Favorite Hot Chicken Salad
Mrs. Albert Aebersold, Lancaster, Ohio

When I first tried this dish at a church luncheon, it reminded me of all the wonderful meals my grandma used to make. My family loves the old-fashioned flavor.

2 cups mayonnaise
1/4 cup lemon juice
5 cups cubed cooked chicken
1 cup sliced celery
1 cup cooked rice
1 cup slivered almonds, toasted
1/4 cup minced onion
1 jar (2 ounces) diced pimientos, drained
1 cup (4 ounces) shredded cheddar cheese
1-1/2 cups crushed potato chips

In a large bowl, mix mayonnaise and lemon juice until smooth. Add chicken, celery, rice, almonds, onion and pimientos; mix well. Spoon into a greased 13-in. x 9-in. x 2-in. baking dish. Sprinkle with cheese and potato chips. Bake, uncovered, at 325° for 30-35 minutes or until bubbly. **Yield:** 6-8 servings.

Overnight Noodle Toss
Edna Hoffman, Hebron, Indiana

Whenever I anticipate a busy day ahead of me, I assemble this dish the night before. Then, the next day, I can serve a super supper without a lot of fuss.

1 can (10-3/4 ounces) condensed cream of mushroom soup, undiluted
1 can (10-3/4 ounces) condensed cream of celery soup, undiluted
2 cups milk
1 package (10 ounces) frozen mixed vegetables, thawed
1 box (7 ounces) elbow macaroni
1 jar (4-1/2 ounces) sliced mushrooms, drained
1/2 pound process American cheese, cubed
3 hard-cooked eggs, chopped
2 cups cubed cooked chicken
1/4 cup chopped onion
1/2 teaspoon salt
1/2 teaspoon pepper

In a large bowl, combine soups and milk until smooth. Add remaining ingredients; mix well. Pour into a greased 13-in. x 9-in. x 2-in. baking dish. Cover and refrigerate 8 hours or overnight. Remove from the refrigerator 30 minutes before baking. Cover and bake at 350° for 50 minutes. Uncover; bake 25-30 minutes more or until bubbly. **Yield:** 6-8 servings.

Chicken Garden Medley

Dohreen Winkler, Howell, Michigan
(PICTURED AT LEFT)

After my family sampled this dish at a friend's house, it quickly became a favorite—especially with our teenage daughters, who request it at least once a week!

- 1 pound boneless skinless chicken breasts, cut into strips
- 1 garlic clove, minced
- 1/4 cup butter *or* margarine, *divided*
- 1 small yellow squash, julienned
- 1 small zucchini, julienned
- 1/2 cup *each* julienned green and sweet red pepper
- 1/4 cup thinly sliced onion
- 2 tablespoons all-purpose flour
- 1/2 teaspoon salt
- 1/4 teaspoon pepper
- 3/4 cup chicken broth
- 1/2 cup half-and-half cream
- 8 ounces angel hair pasta, cooked and drained
- 2 tablespoons shredded Parmesan cheese

In a large skillet over medium-high heat, saute chicken and garlic in 2 tablespoons butter for 10-12 minutes or until chicken juices run clear. Add vegetables; cook until crisp-tender; set aside. In a small saucepan, melt remaining butter. Add flour, salt and pepper; stir to form a smooth paste. Gradually add broth, stirring constantly. Bring to a boil; cook for 2 minutes or until thickened. Stir in cream and heat through. Pour over chicken and vegetables; stir until well mixed. Place pasta in a greased 2-qt. baking dish. Pour chicken mixture over top. Sprinkle with Parmesan cheese. Cover and bake at 350° for 20 minutes; uncover and bake 10 minutes longer. **Yield:** 4-6 servings.

Green Bean Casserole with Biscuits

Sandra Wanamaker, Germansville, Pennsylvania

My husband is a real "meat and potatoes" man, but he'll always try the various foods I prepare. He especially enjoys this creamy casserole served over hot homemade biscuits.

- 1 can (10-3/4 ounces) condensed cream of chicken soup, undiluted
- 1 can (10-3/4 ounces) condensed cheddar cheese soup, undiluted
- 1 can (5 ounces) evaporated milk
- 3 cups frozen green beans, thawed and drained
- 3 cups diced cooked chicken
- 1 cup chopped celery
- 2 tablespoons chopped onion
- 1 jar (2 ounces) diced pimientos, drained
- 1/2 cup chow mein noodles
- 1/2 cup slivered almonds, toasted

SINGULAR SENSATION. *Pictured at left, Chicken Garden Medley (recipe on this page).*

- 1/2 teaspoon salt
- 1/4 teaspoon pepper
- 1/2 cup french-fried onions

Hot biscuits

In a large bowl, stir soups and milk until smooth. Add the next nine ingredients. Spoon into a greased 2-1/2-qt. baking dish. Bake, uncovered, at 350° for 40 minutes or until bubbly. Sprinkle with onions; bake 10 minutes longer. Serve over biscuits. **Yield:** 4-6 servings.

Chicken Tamale Pie

Diane Thayer, Iowa City, Iowa

This pie has become a standby for weekday suppers. The zesty filling satisfies our craving for Mexican food. And the kids like the crust, which tastes like corn muffins.

- 1 box (8-1/2 ounces) corn bread/muffin mix
- 1 egg, beaten
- 1/3 cup milk
- 1/2 cup shredded cheddar cheese
- 1 can (10-3/4 ounces) condensed cream of chicken soup, undiluted
- 2 cups cubed cooked chicken
- 1 cup frozen corn, thawed
- 1/2 cup chopped green onions
- 1 can (4 ounces) chopped green chilies
- 1 garlic clove, minced
- 1/2 to 3/4 teaspoon chili powder

In a mixing bowl, combine muffin mix, egg and milk; add cheese. Spread in the bottom and up the sides of a greased 9-in. pie plate. In a saucepan, combine soup, chicken, corn, onions, chilies, garlic and chili powder; heat through. Immediately pour into crust. Bake at 400° for 20-25 minutes or until crust is golden and filling is hot. **Yield:** 6 servings.

Easy Vegetable Casserole

Gertrude Bartnick, Portage, Wisconsin

This hearty dish combines chicken and an assortment of vegetables. It can be put together in a snap...a real plus for any busy cook.

- 2 cups cubed cooked chicken
- 8 ounces frozen small onions, thawed and drained
- 1 package (10 ounces) frozen mixed vegetables, thawed and drained
- 1 can (4 ounces) mushroom stems and pieces, drained
- 1 can (10-3/4 ounces) condensed cream of chicken soup, undiluted
- 1/2 teaspoon dried thyme
- 1 cup crushed potato chips

In a bowl, combine chicken, onions, mixed vegetables, mushrooms, soup and thyme. Pour into a greased 8-in. square baking dish. Sprinkle with chips. Bake, uncovered, at 350° for 50-55 minutes or until bubbly. **Yield:** 4-6 servings.

Festive Family Fare

These recipes prove elegant entrees can be easy to prepare. And they're guaranteed to make meals with friends and family even more inviting.

Chicken and Asparagus
Janet Hill, Sacramento, California
(PICTURED AT LEFT)

With this recipe, you'll see fancy foods don't necessarily mean a lot of fuss. These "bundles" are prepared in no time and bake in the oven for a quick tasty dinner.

✓ This tasty dish uses less sugar, salt and fat. Recipe includes *Diabetic Exchanges*.

  4 boneless skinless chicken breast halves
 24 fresh asparagus spears, trimmed
1/3 cup Italian salad dressing
  2 teaspoons soy sauce
1/2 teaspoon ground ginger
1/2 teaspoon salt, optional
1/8 teaspoon pepper
  2 tablespoons sesame seeds
Hot cooked white and wild rice blend, optional

Cut each chicken breast half into 1/2-in.-wide strips. Wrap two or three strips around three asparagus spears. Repeat with the remaining chicken and asparagus. Arrange in a greased 13-in. x 9-in. x 2-in. baking dish. Combine salad dressing, soy sauce, ginger, salt if desired and pepper. Pour over the chicken bundles. Cover and bake at 350° for 25 minutes. Uncover; sprinkle with sesame seeds and bake 15 minutes longer or until chicken juices run clear. Serve over rice if desired. **Yield:** 4 servings. **Diabetic Exchanges:** One serving (prepared with reduced-fat salad dressing and low-sodium soy sauce, without added salt and served without rice) equals 3 lean meat, 1-1/2 vegetable; also, 222 calories, 283 mg sodium, 73 mg cholesterol, 7 gm carbohydrate, 31 gm protein, 8 gm fat.

Fruit-Glazed Roast Chicken
Lynn Stromquist, Fridley, Minnesota
(PICTURED AT LEFT)

Whenever I want to serve a special meal with a little flair, this is the recipe I reach for. To round out the dinner, I serve oven-roasted potatoes and a salad.

  2 lemons, quartered
  2 broiler-fryer chickens (3 to 3-1/2 pounds *each*)
3/4 cup dried apricots
1/3 cup chicken broth
  3 tablespoons cider vinegar
  3 tablespoons brown sugar
  2 tablespoons lemon juice

SPECIAL-OCCASION SUPPERS. *Pictured at left, top to bottom: Fruit-Glazed Roast Chicken and Chicken and Asparagus (recipes on this page).*

---

  2 tablespoons golden raisins
1/4 teaspoon ground ginger
1/4 teaspoon salt
1/2 cup sugar
1/2 cup water
  2 cans (16 ounces *each*) pear halves, drained
  1 can (16 ounces) peach halves, drained
  1 can (16 ounces) apricot halves, drained
  1 cup pitted prunes
Lemon leaves, optional

Place four lemon quarters in body cavity of each chicken; close cavities with skewers or string. Place chickens, breast side up, on a rack in a large roasting pan; bake at 375° for 1-1/2 hours. Meanwhile, in a food processor or blender, combine dried apricots, broth, vinegar, brown sugar, lemon juice, raisins, ginger and salt. Process until smooth; set aside. In a small saucepan, bring sugar and water to a boil over medium-high heat. Reduce heat to medium; cook, uncovered, for 7 minutes. In a large bowl, combine pears, peaches, apricots and prunes; pour hot syrup over fruit. Let stand 10 minutes; drain and set aside. Remove chickens from oven; spread thickly with pureed apricot mixture. Return to the oven for 10-15 minutes or until chicken juices run clear. Remove from oven and let stand 10 minutes. Prepare gravy from pan drippings if desired. Place chickens on serving platter; spoon fruit mixture around chickens. Garnish with lemon leaves if desired. Serve with gravy if desired. **Yield:** 8 servings.

Dijon Chicken
Wanda Maxwell, West Columbia, Texas

This dish was created by our son, who is known by friends and family to be a great cook. Everyone who tries these delicious chicken breasts comments on the zesty mustard flavor.

1/3 cup Dijon mustard
1/3 cup sour cream
  6 boneless skinless chicken breast halves
1-1/4 cups Italian-style bread crumbs
 24 stuffed green *or* pitted ripe olives
1/4 cup butter *or* margarine, melted
  1 tablespoon fresh lemon juice
1/8 teaspoon cayenne pepper
  6 lemon slices

In a shallow bowl, combine mustard and sour cream. Dip chicken in mixture, coating both sides, then roll in bread crumbs. Place four olives in the center of each chicken breast; fold in half. Place in an ungreased 11-in. x 7-in. x 2-in. baking dish. Combine butter, lemon juice and cayenne pepper; drizzle over chicken. Place a slice of lemon on each chicken breast. Bake, uncovered, at 325° for 40-45 minutes or until juices run clear. **Yield:** 6 servings.

Lemon Almond Chicken
Nancy Schmidt, Delhi, California

"Melt-in-your-mouth tender" is how folks describe this golden chicken with a delicate lemon sauce. The almonds add a subtle nutty flavor everyone enjoys.

1-1/4 cups all-purpose flour
2-3/4 teaspoons salt
  3/4 teaspoon pepper
    6 large boneless skinless chicken breast halves
    2 eggs, beaten
    2 tablespoons cooking oil
  1/4 cup plus 2 tablespoons butter *or* margarine, *divided*
    1 tablespoon minced green onions
    1 garlic clove, minced
1-1/2 cups chicken broth
  1/2 cup dry white wine *or* ginger ale
    3 tablespoons fresh lemon juice
  1/2 cup slivered almonds, toasted
Minced fresh parsley
    1 lemon, thinly sliced

In a shallow bowl or large resealable plastic bag, combine flour, salt and pepper; set aside 1/4 cup for sauce. Dredge chicken in remaining flour mixture, then dip in eggs. Heat oil and 2 tablespoons butter in a large skillet over medium-high heat. Add chicken; saute until golden brown on both sides. Drain on paper towels. Place in a greased 13-in. x 9-in. x 2-in. baking dish. For sauce, melt remaining butter in a small saucepan. Add onions and garlic; cook for 1 minute. Stir in reserved flour mixture; cook and stir for 1 minute. Gradually add broth, ginger ale and lemon juice; cook for 2 minutes or until slightly thickened and bubbly. Pour over chicken. Bake, uncovered, at 375° for 20-30 minutes. Top with almonds, parsley and lemon. Serve immediately. **Yield:** 6 servings.

Spinach-Stuffed Chicken Breasts
Joyce Brown, Genesee, Idaho

Combining spinach and chicken in one dish is a favorite standby for country cooks. The addition of ricotta and Parmesan cheeses makes this chicken extraordinary.

    1 medium onion, chopped
    1 tablespoon butter *or* margarine
    3 tablespoons olive *or* vegetable oil, *divided*
    1 package (10 ounces) frozen chopped spinach, thawed and well drained
  1/2 cup ricotta cheese
  1/2 cup grated Parmesan cheese
    1 teaspoon dried basil
  1/2 teaspoon salt
  1/4 teaspoon pepper
    6 chicken breast halves (bone in)
  1/4 teaspoon dried thyme
Additional salt to taste

In a large skillet, saute onion in butter and 1 tablespoon oil until tender. Add spinach; cook until heated through and any moisture has evaporated. Remove from the heat; cool. Stir in cheeses, basil, salt and pepper. Loosen skin on one side of each chicken breast. Place 1/3 cup filling under skin; place chicken with filling side up in an ungreased 13-in. x 9-in. x 2-in. baking dish. Drizzle with remaining oil. Sprinkle with thyme and salt. Bake, uncovered, at 375° for 45 minutes or until chicken juices run clear. **Yield:** 6 servings.

Chicken Florentine
Anne Yaeger, Minneapolis, Minnesota

These individual chicken breast rolls may take some time to prepare, but their outstanding flavor makes it well worth it. Get ready to copy the recipe for all who taste it!

 10 boneless skinless chicken breast halves
  2 tablespoons honey
  1 package (10 ounces) frozen chopped spinach, thawed and well drained
  2 cups (8 ounces) shredded cheddar cheese
1/3 cup all-purpose flour
  2 teaspoons garlic salt
  1 teaspoon pepper
  1 egg
1/3 cup milk
  1 cup dry bread crumbs
Cooking oil for deep-fat frying

Pound chicken breasts to 1/4-in. thickness; brush each with honey. Combine spinach and cheese; place about 2 tablespoons in the center of each chicken breast. Fold long sides over filling; fold ends up and secure with a toothpick. Place, seam side down, in a shallow pan. Cover and refrigerate for several hours. In a shallow bowl, combine flour, garlic salt and pepper. In another shallow bowl, beat egg and milk. Dredge chicken in flour mixture, dip in egg mixture and roll in bread crumbs. Heat oil in a deep-fat fryer to 350°. Fry chicken, several rolls at a time, for 1-1/2 minutes or until golden brown. Place in an ungreased 13-in. x 9-in. x 2-in. baking dish. Bake, uncovered, at 350° for 30 minutes or until juices run clear. Remove toothpicks before serving. **Yield:** 6-8 servings.

Cran-Apple Chicken
Patricia Litchfield, Sheffield, Massachusetts

Here's an easy-to-prepare meal you'll enjoy year-round. The fruity glaze really complements the chicken, and the crumbled raisin bagel in the stuffing is a unique touch.

    2 cups corn muffin crumbs
    1 day-old raisin bagel, crumbled
  1/2 cup applesauce
  1/4 cup Grape-Nuts cereal
  1/4 cup hot water
    2 tablespoons butter *or* margarine, melted
1-1/2 teaspoons poultry seasoning
  1/2 teaspoon salt
  1/2 teaspoon dried minced onion
  1/4 teaspoon ground nutmeg

1/4 teaspoon pepper
1-1/4 pounds boneless skinless chicken breast halves
GLAZE:
   1/4 cup whole-berry cranberry sauce
   1/4 cup applesauce
    2 tablespoons honey
    2 tablespoons butter *or* margarine

In a medium bowl, combine first 11 ingredients; toss well. Spoon into a greased 11-in. x 7-in. x 2-in. baking dish. Cut each chicken breast half into four pieces; arrange over stuffing. Combine glaze ingredients in a small saucepan. Cook over medium-low heat until butter is melted; spoon over chicken. Cover and bake at 400° for 25 minutes. Uncover and bake 5 minutes longer or until chicken juices run clear. **Yield:** 4-6 servings.

Raspberry Basil Chicken
Isabelle Pederson, Valley City, North Dakota

This recipe turns ordinary raspberry jam into a sweet succulent glaze. With its attractive color and delicious flavor, this chicken is great to serve family and friends.

    1 broiler-fryer chicken (3-1/2 to 4 pounds), cut up
    1 teaspoon dried basil
    1 teaspoon salt
   1/2 teaspoon pepper
    1 medium onion, thinly sliced
    1 cup seedless raspberry jam

Place chicken in a greased 13-in. x 9-in. x 2-in. baking dish. Sprinkle with basil, salt and pepper. Top with onion. Cover and bake at 375° for 30 minutes. Drain pan juices and reserve 1/2 cup (add water to make 1/2 cup if necessary). Add jam; pour over chicken. Bake, uncovered, basting occasionally, for 25 minutes or until chicken juices run clear. **Yield:** 4-6 servings.

Cheesy Chicken Crepes
Martha McCool, Jacksonville, Florida

Our family loves all kinds of outdoor activities, including fishing, hunting and swimming. Indoors, my favorite pastime is cooking delicious dishes like these creamy crepes.

CREPES:
    3 eggs
  2/3 cup all-purpose flour
  1/2 teaspoon salt
    1 cup milk
FILLING:
    3 cups thinly sliced fresh mushrooms (8 ounces)
  1/3 cup sliced green onions
    2 tablespoons butter *or* margarine
  3/4 cup mayonnaise
  1/2 cup all-purpose flour

  1/2 teaspoon dried rosemary, crushed
  1/2 teaspoon salt
  1/2 teaspoon pepper
  1/4 teaspoon garlic powder
    2 cups milk, *divided*
1-1/2 cups (6 ounces) shredded cheddar cheese, *divided*
    2 cups chopped cooked chicken

In a medium bowl, beat eggs. Add flour, salt and milk; stir until smooth. Let stand 15 minutes. Heat a lightly greased 8-in. skillet; add 1/4 cup batter, lift and turn pan to cover bottom. Cook until lightly browned on one side. Repeat with remaining batter, greasing skillet as needed. Stack crepes with waxed paper between them. For filling, saute mushrooms and onions in butter in a large skillet until mushrooms are tender; set aside. In a 2-qt. saucepan, combine mayonnaise, flour, rosemary, salt, pepper and garlic powder. Cook over medium-low heat for 2-3 minutes. Gradually stir in 1-1/2 cups milk. Cook, stirring constantly, until thickened and bubbly. Add 1 cup cheese and stir until melted. Remove from the heat; add chicken and the mushroom mixture. Spoon 1/3 cup down the center of each crepe. Roll up and place, seam side down, in a greased 13-in. x 9-in. x 2-in. baking dish. Heat remaining milk and cheese, stirring until cheese is melted. Pour over crepes. Bake, uncovered, at 350° for 15-20 minutes or until heated through. **Yield:** 6 servings.

Pecan Poultry Stuffing
Mary Krietemeyer, Fort Jennings, Ohio

I recently added this recipe to my extensive collection and have already made it quite a few times. The chicken is always moist, and the pecans add a festive crunch to the stuffing.

  1/4 cup *each* finely chopped carrot, celery and onion
  1/2 cup butter *or* margarine, *divided*
    1 teaspoon poultry seasoning
  1/4 teaspoon celery salt
  1/4 teaspoon pepper
2-1/2 cups unseasoned stuffing croutons
  2/3 cup chopped pecans
  1/2 to 3/4 cup chicken broth
    6 chicken breast halves (bone in)
    1 tablespoon lemon juice
Salt to taste
Paprika

In a large skillet, saute carrot, celery and onion in 1 tablespoon butter until crisp-tender. Add poultry seasoning, celery salt and pepper; mix well. Remove from the heat. Add croutons and pecans; toss. Stir in enough broth to moisten. Divide stuffing into six equal amounts. Loosen skin on one side of each chicken breast. Place stuffing under skin. Arrange chicken with stuffing side up in an ungreased 13-in. x 9-in. x 2-in. baking dish. Melt remaining butter. Stir in lemon juice; drizzle over chicken. Sprinkle with salt and paprika. Cover and bake at 350° for 45 minutes. Uncover and bake 10 minutes longer or until chicken is browned and juices run clear. **Yield:** 6 servings.

Chicken and Ham Roll-Ups
Karen Mawhinney, Teeswater, Ontario

I first started making these easy roll-ups as a way to use left-over chicken. My family raved about them so much that I now frequently serve them when entertaining.

```
        3  cups cooked rice
    1-1/2  cups chopped cooked chicken
        1  can (10-3/4 ounces) condensed cream of
           chicken soup, undiluted, divided
      1/4  cup finely chopped celery
        1  green onion, thinly sliced
      1/4  teaspoon pepper, divided
        6  slices fully cooked ham
      1/4  cup sour cream or plain yogurt
      1/4  cup milk
      1/4  teaspoon dried thyme
      1/2  cup shredded Swiss or mozzarella cheese
```
Paprika *or* additional chopped green onion

Spread rice in a greased 11-in. x 7-in. x 2-in. microwave-safe baking dish; set aside. In a medium bowl, combine chicken, 1/3 cup soup, celery, onion and 1/8 teaspoon pepper. Place 1/4 cup on each ham slice and roll up. Secure with a toothpick if necessary. Place ham rolls, seam side down, on top of rice. Combine sour cream, milk, thyme and remaining soup and pepper; spoon over rolls. Cover and microwave on high, turning dish halfway through cooking time, for 10-14 minutes or until heated through. Sprinkle with cheese and paprika or onion; cover and let stand 5 minutes. Remove toothpicks before serving. **Yield:** 4-6 servings. **Editor's Note:** This recipe was tested in a 700-watt microwave. Roll-ups may be baked in a conventional oven at 350° for 25-30 minutes or until heated through.

Bacon-Topped Chicken Breasts
Mary Engelmeyer, West Point, Nebraska

Even people who aren't fond of spinach will become fans after they taste this dish, with its bacon and rich sauce.

```
        3  cups sliced fresh mushrooms (8 ounces)
        1  cup chopped green pepper
        1  medium onion, chopped
        2  tablespoons cooking oil
        1  package (10 ounces) frozen chopped spinach,
           thawed and well drained
        1  can (10-3/4 ounces) condensed creamy
           chicken mushroom soup, undiluted
        1  cup (8 ounces) sour cream
        1  teaspoon paprika
      1/2  teaspoon salt
      1/4  teaspoon pepper
        6  chicken breast halves (bone in)
        4  bacon strips, cooked and crumbled
```
Hot cooked noodles, optional

In a large skillet, saute mushrooms, green pepper and onion in oil until tender. Add spinach; cook for 2 minutes. Add soup, sour cream, paprika, salt and pepper;

heat through. Spread in the bottom of a greased 13-in. x 9-in. x 2-in. baking dish. Arrange chicken on top. Bake, uncovered, at 350° for 50-60 minutes. Sprinkle with bacon and return to the oven for 5 minutes. Serve over noodles if desired. **Yield:** 6 servings.

Mexican-Style Chicken Kiev
Lenita Brouillette, Las Vegas, Nevada

When we have company for dinner, I like to use recipes that can be assembled hours in advance so I have more time to visit. This chicken dish truly fills the bill!

```
        4  large boneless skinless chicken breast halves
        1  can (4 ounces) chopped green chilies, drained
        2  ounces Monterey Jack cheese, cut into 4 strips
      1/4  cup fine dry bread crumbs
        2  tablespoons grated Parmesan cheese
    3-1/2  teaspoons chili powder
      1/4  teaspoon salt
      1/8  teaspoon ground cumin
        4  tablespoons butter or margarine, melted, divided
        1  cup picante sauce
      1/2  cup cold water
        2  teaspoons cornstarch
      1/2  teaspoon chicken bouillon granules
```

Pound chicken to 1/4-in. thickness. Put about 2 tablespoons chilies and one strip of Monterey Jack cheese on long end of each chicken breast. Fold in sides and ends; secure with a toothpick. In a shallow bowl, combine the crumbs, Parmesan cheese, chili powder, salt and cumin. Dip chicken in 3 tablespoons butter, then roll in crumb mixture. Place chicken rolls, seam side down, in an ungreased 11-in. x 7-in. x 2-in. baking dish. Drizzle with remaining butter. Cover and refrigerate at least 4 hours. Bake, uncovered, at 400° for 20-25 minutes or until chicken is tender. Meanwhile, combine picante sauce, water, cornstarch and bouillon in a small saucepan. Bring to a boil over medium heat; cook and stir 1 minute. Remove toothpicks from chicken and serve with sauce. **Yield:** 4 servings.

Chicken with Cranberry Compote
Colette Jaworski, Buford, Georgia

Everyone always said this chicken was a winner, and I guess they were right. I became a finalist in a national chicken cooking contest after submitting this recipe!

```
        4  boneless skinless chicken breast halves
        2  tablespoons fresh lemon juice
        2  tablespoons vegetable oil
      1/2  teaspoon salt
      1/4  teaspoon pepper
      1/4  cup dried cranberries
        1  cup boiling water
        4  tablespoons butter or margarine, divided
      1/2  cup chopped celery
      1/4  cup diced red onion
      1/2  cup chopped tart apple
      1/4  cup cranberry juice
```

3 tablespoons apple juice
1 tablespoon red wine vinegar
1/4 teaspoon ground coriander
1/8 teaspoon ground allspice

Place chicken in a large shallow bowl. Combine lemon juice, oil, salt and pepper; pour over chicken. Cover and refrigerate. Meanwhile, place cranberries in a small bowl. Cover with boiling water and let stand for 15 minutes. In a 2-qt. saucepan, melt 2 tablespoons butter over medium-high heat. Add celery and onion; saute until onion is tender. Reduce heat to medium. Drain cranberries; add to celery mixture with apple. Stir in cranberry juice, apple juice and vinegar. Cook, stirring constantly, for 5 minutes or until liquid is reduced by half. Stir in coriander and allspice. Cover and keep warm. Drain chicken, discarding marinade. In a large skillet, melt remaining butter over medium-high heat. Add chicken and cook 5 minutes or until lightly browned. Turn; cover and reduce heat to low. Cook 10 minutes longer or until juices run clear. Place chicken on a serving platter and top with cranberry compote. **Yield:** 4 servings.

Sausage-Stuffed Chicken
Kelly Kendlehart, Allen, Texas

I came up with this entree one day when I was looking for something new and interesting to serve guests. The sausage makes the chicken even more hearty and satisfying.

2 packages (10 ounces *each*) frozen broccoli spears, thawed and drained
1 pound bulk pork sausage
1/2 cup chopped onion
1/2 cup shredded cheddar cheese
1/2 cup dry bread crumbs
Salt and pepper to taste
1 egg
8 boneless skinless chicken breast halves
1 can (10-3/4 ounces) condensed creamy chicken mushroom soup, undiluted

Place broccoli in an ungreased 13-in. x 9-in. x 2-in. baking dish; set aside. In a large skillet, brown sausage and onion until sausage is no longer pink; drain. Remove from the heat. Add cheese, crumbs, salt, pepper and egg; mix well. Flatten each chicken breast to 1/4-in. thickness. Place about 1/3 cup mixture down center of each chicken breast. Fold long ends over filling; fold ends up and secure with a toothpick. Place chicken, seam side down, on top of broccoli; spread soup over all. Bake, uncovered, at 350° for 40-50 minutes. Remove toothpicks before serving. **Yield:** 8 servings.

Curried Chicken and Rice
Tammi Lewis, Bellevue, Ohio

Curry sauce makes this version of chicken and rice stand out from all the others. Your guests will think you spent hours in the kitchen preparing this impressive dish!

1 cup chicken broth
1 teaspoon curry powder

1/2 teaspoon paprika
1 box (6 ounces) long grain and wild rice mix
3 cups sliced fresh mushrooms (8 ounces)
10 ounces fresh pearl onions, cooked according to package directions
1/2 medium green pepper, julienned
1 broiler-fryer chicken (3-1/2 to 4 pounds), cut up
CURRY SAUCE:
1 carton (8 ounces) plain yogurt
1/2 cup ricotta cheese
1/3 cup chutney
1 tablespoon all-purpose flour
2 teaspoons curry powder
2 tablespoons slivered almonds

In an ungreased 13-in. x 9-in. x 2-in. baking dish, combine broth, curry powder, paprika and seasoning mix from the rice. Top with rice, mushrooms, onions and green pepper. Arrange chicken pieces on top. Cover and bake at 425° for 50 minutes. Meanwhile, in a blender or food processor, combine yogurt, ricotta cheese, chutney, flour and curry powder. Process until smooth; pour over chicken. Sprinkle with almonds. Increase oven temperature to 475°. Bake, uncovered, for 5-10 minutes. **Yield:** 4-6 servings.

Chicken Lasagna Rolls
Virginia Shaw, Modesto, California

Whether for an everyday meal or special occasion, this is a fun and creative way to serve lasagna. Chicken and almonds add a tasty new twist.

1/2 cup chopped onion
1/2 cup chopped sweet red pepper
1/2 cup chopped almonds
1/3 cup butter *or* margarine
1/2 cup cornstarch
1-1/2 teaspoons salt
2 cans (10-3/4 ounces *each*) chicken broth
2 cups chopped cooked chicken
1 package (10 ounces) frozen chopped spinach, thawed and well drained
1/4 teaspoon pepper
1/4 teaspoon ground nutmeg
10 lasagna noodles, cooked and drained
2 cups milk
1 cup (4 ounces) shredded Swiss cheese, *divided*
1/4 cup dry white wine *or* water

In a 3-qt. saucepan, saute onion, red pepper and almonds in butter over low heat until onion is softened and almonds are toasted. Stir in cornstarch and salt. Cook over low heat for 1 minute, stirring constantly. Slowly stir in broth; cook and stir over medium heat until thickened and bubbly. Transfer half of the sauce to a medium bowl; stir in chicken, spinach, pepper and nutmeg. Spread about 3 tablespoons over each lasagna noodle. Roll up and place, seam side down, in a greased 11-in. x 7-in. x 2-in. baking dish. Add milk, 1/2 cup Swiss cheese and water or wine to remaining sauce. Cook and stir over medium heat until thickened and bubbly. Pour over noodles. Bake, uncovered, at 350° for 20 minutes. Sprinkle with remaining cheese; return to the oven for 5 minutes or until cheese is melted. **Yield:** 5 servings.

Hot Off the Grill

When you fire up the grill for the mouth-watering sizzle of this warm-weather fare, flavorful fun with family and friends is sure to follow.

Honey-Mustard Chicken

Heidi Holmes, Renton, Washington

(PICTURED AT LEFT)

If my family had their wish, I'd serve chicken on the grill every night. This sweet and tangy glaze is an appealing alternative to traditional tomato-based sauces.

    1 cup pineapple juice
  3/4 cup honey
  1/2 cup Dijon mustard
    1 teaspoon ground ginger
    2 tablespoons cornstarch
  1/4 cup cold water
    1 broiler-fryer chicken (3-1/2 to 4 pounds), cut up

In a small saucepan, combine pineapple juice, honey, mustard and ginger; bring to a boil. Combine cornstarch and water; whisk into honey mixture. Cook, stirring constantly, for 2-3 minutes or until thickened. Reserve 3/4 cup to serve with chicken if desired. Brush chicken with remaining glaze. Grill, covered, over medium-low coals for 30 minutes. Turn chicken; brush again with glaze. Grill, uncovered, for 20 minutes or until juices run clear. Serve with reserved glaze if desired. **Yield:** 4 servings.

Dad's Best Barbecue

Connie Will, Edinburg, Virginia

(PICTURED AT LEFT)

Whenever I prepare this great chicken, I fondly remember my father. He would make his "famous" chicken frequently for picnics and other functions.

    2 cups vinegar
    1 cup vegetable oil
    1 cup ketchup
  1/2 cup tomato juice
    2 to 3 tablespoons hot pepper sauce
    1 tablespoon poultry seasoning
4-1/2 teaspoons salt
1-1/2 teaspoons pepper
  3/4 teaspoon garlic powder
    6 broiler-fryer chicken halves

In a large bowl, combine the first nine ingredients. Reserve 1 cup for basting chicken; cover. Pour remaining marinade over chicken in a large roasting pan. Cover and refrigerate for 4 hours. Drain, discarding marinade. Grill chicken, covered, over low coals, turning and brushing with reserved marinade several times, for 60-75 minutes or until juices run clear. **Yield:** 6 servings.

Mustard-Lover's Grilled Chicken

Leslie Bernard, Kingwood, Texas

(PICTURED AT LEFT)

I'm a big fan of all types of mustard. So I knew I had to try this recipe. My family loves the unique robust sauce.

  1/4 cup butter *or* margarine
1-1/3 cups yellow mustard
  1/4 cup vinegar
  1/2 teaspoon salt
  1/2 teaspoon pepper
    2 garlic cloves, minced
    3 drops hot pepper sauce
3-1/2 pounds chicken legs *or* thighs
Cucumber slices, optional
Hot peppers, optional

In a small saucepan, melt butter over low heat. Stir in mustard, vinegar, salt, pepper, garlic and hot pepper sauce. Cook and stir until thoroughly combined; remove from the heat. Grill chicken, covered, over medium coals, turning occasionally, for 20 minutes. Brush with sauce. Continue basting and turning chicken several times for an additional 10 minutes or until juices run clear. Garnish with cucumbers and peppers if desired. **Yield:** 6-8 servings.

Garlic-Lime Chicken

Doris Carnahan, Lincoln, Arkansas

After tending the farm and growing our own produce, I don't have much time left for cooking. I've found this easy-to-prepare chicken is ideal for my many hectic days.

✓ This tasty dish uses less sugar, salt and fat. Recipe includes *Diabetic Exchanges*.

  1/3 cup soy sauce
  1/4 cup fresh lime juice
    1 tablespoon Worcestershire sauce
  1/2 teaspoon dry mustard
    2 garlic cloves, minced
    6 boneless skinless chicken breast halves
  1/2 teaspoon pepper

Combine first five ingredients. Place chicken in a large resealable plastic bag or glass bowl; pour sauce over chicken. Cover or close bag and refrigerate for at least 30 minutes. Drain, discarding marinade. Place chicken on grill and sprinkle with pepper. Grill, uncovered, over medium-low coals, turning several times, for 12-15 minutes or until juices run clear. **Yield:** 6 servings. **Diabetic Exchanges:** One serving (prepared with low-sodium soy sauce) equals 3 lean meat; also, 147 calories, 166 mg sodium, 73 mg cholesterol, 1 gm carbohydrate, 27 gm protein, 3 gm fat.

FINGER-LICKING GOODIES. *Pictured at left, top to bottom: Honey-Mustard Chicken, Dad's Best Barbecue and Mustard-Lover's Grilled Chicken (all recipes on this page).*

Grilled Curry Chicken
Schelby Thompson, Dover, Delaware

We're fortunate to have mild winters, so we fire up the grill throughout the year. Of all the meals I prepare, my family enjoys this slightly spicy chicken the most.

✓ This tasty dish uses less sugar, salt and fat. Recipe includes *Diabetic Exchanges*.

- 1 broiler-fryer chicken (3 to 3-1/2 pounds), cut up and skin removed
- 1 carton (8 ounces) plain yogurt
- 1 medium onion, quartered
- 2 garlic cloves
- 2 tablespoons curry powder
- 1 tablespoon paprika
- 1-1/2 teaspoons salt, optional
- 1/4 teaspoon ground red pepper

Pierce chicken liberally with a fork, then make 1/2-in.-deep diagonal cuts, about 1 in. apart, in the meat. Place in a large resealable plastic bag or a glass 13-in. x 9-in. x 2-in. baking dish; set aside. In a blender or food processor, combine yogurt, onion, garlic, curry, paprika, salt if desired and red pepper; process until smooth. Reserve 1/4 cup for basting; cover and chill. Pour remaining mixture over chicken; turn to coat. Cover or close bag and refrigerate for at least 8 hours. Drain, discarding marinade. Grill chicken, covered, over medium coals, turning and basting with reserved yogurt mixture every 5 minutes, for 30-40 minutes or until juices run clear. **Yield:** 4 servings. **Diabetic Exchanges:** One serving (prepared with nonfat yogurt and without added salt) equals 4 lean meat, 1/2 vegetable; also, 235 calories, 123 mg sodium, 96 mg cholesterol, 5 gm carbohydrate, 38 gm protein, 6 gm fat.

Campfire Casseroles
Julie Wilson, Fort Collins, Colorado

Because they make individual portions, you can tailor these chicken and vegetable "casseroles" to suit everyone's tastes. They're great when camping with a group.

- 6 skinless chicken breast halves (bone in)
- 6 sheets heavy-duty aluminum foil (18 inches x 12 inches)
- 6 carrots, sliced 1/4 inch thick
- 3 medium potatoes, sliced 1/4 inch thick
- 1/2 pound fresh mushrooms, quartered
- 1 medium onion, sliced
- 6 tablespoons butter *or* margarine
- 1 can (10-3/4 ounces) condensed cream of chicken soup, undiluted

Salt and pepper to taste

Place each chicken breast in the center of a piece of foil. Divide carrots, potatoes, mushrooms and onion equally and place on top and around each piece of chicken. Top each with 1 tablespoon butter and about 2 tablespoons soup. Sprinkle with salt and pepper. Bring opposite long edges of foil together over the top of each breast and fold down several times. Fold the short ends toward the food and crimp tightly to prevent leaks. Grill, covered, over medium-low coals for 50-60 minutes or until chick-

en juices run clear and potatoes are tender. To serve, unwrap packets and spoon contents onto individual plates. **Yield:** 6 servings.

Mexican Grilled Chicken
Lisa Ousley, Willard, Ohio

As a full-time homemaker and mother of two, I'm thrilled to find dishes that can be assembled and cooked in no time—like this chicken. Any leftovers are even better the next day.

- 1/2 cup mayonnaise
- 3 tablespoons fresh lime juice
- 1 envelope taco seasoning mix
- 8 boneless skinless chicken breast halves

In a small bowl, mix together mayonnaise, lime juice and taco seasoning until smooth. Place chicken on grill over medium coals. Sear one side; turn and brush with sauce. Grill, uncovered, for 6 minutes; turn and brush with sauce. Grill another 6 minutes or until chicken juices run clear. **Yield:** 6-8 servings.

Caribbean Delight
Leigh Ann Grady, Murray, Kentucky

When hot summer nights drive me out of the kitchen, I head for the grill with this recipe. Along with a salad, my family loves this not-so-subtle spicy chicken.

- 2 tablespoons minced onion
- 2 garlic cloves, minced
- 1/4 cup butter *or* margarine
- 1/3 cup vinegar
- 1/3 cup fresh lime juice
- 1/4 cup sugar
- 2 tablespoons curry powder
- 1 teaspoon salt
- 1/4 to 1/2 teaspoon cayenne pepper
- 6 boneless skinless chicken breast halves

In a small saucepan, saute onion and garlic in butter until tender. Stir in vinegar, lime juice, sugar, curry powder, salt and cayenne pepper. Place chicken in a large resealable plastic bag or glass 13-in. x 9-in. x 2-in. baking dish; cover with sauce. Cover or close bag and refrigerate at least 2 hours. Drain, discarding marinade. Grill chicken, uncovered, over medium coals, turning once, for 10-15 minutes or until juices run clear. **Yield:** 4-6 servings.

15-Minute Marinated Chicken
Pam Shinogle, Arlington, Texas

Whenever I serve this to family and friends, which is quite often, I'm bound to be asked for the recipe. It's a fast and tasty meal that I'm happy to share with others.

✓ This tasty dish uses less sugar, salt and fat. Recipe includes *Diabetic Exchanges*.

- 1/4 cup Dijon mustard
- 2 tablespoons fresh lemon juice
- 1-1/2 teaspoons Worcestershire sauce

1/2 teaspoon dried tarragon
1/4 teaspoon pepper
  4 boneless skinless chicken breast halves

Combine the first five ingredients; spread on both sides of chicken. Place chicken on a plate. Marinate at room temperature for 10-15 minutes or for several hours in the refrigerator. Grill, uncovered, over medium coals, turning once, for 10-15 minutes or until juices run clear. **Yield:** 4 servings. **Diabetic Exchanges:** One serving equals 3 lean meat; also, 161 calories, 287 mg sodium, 73 mg cholesterol, 2 gm carbohydrate, 28 gm protein, 4 gm fat.

Saucy Barbecued Chicken
Charlotte Witherspoon, Detroit, Michigan

My aunt was affectionately called "The Barbecue Queen". As the aroma of her grilled chicken filled the air, folks in town would stop by just to sample her scrumptious food.

  2 cups ketchup
1/2 cup tomato sauce
1/2 cup water
1/2 cup corn syrup
1/2 cup cola
1/4 cup vinegar
1/4 cup butter *or* margarine
1/4 cup steak sauce
  2 tablespoons soy sauce
1-1/2 teaspoons sugar
  1 teaspoon seasoned salt
  1 teaspoon hot pepper sauce
1/2 teaspoon garlic powder
1/2 teaspoon onion powder
1/2 teaspoon liquid smoke
  1 broiler-fryer chicken (3 to 3-1/2 pounds), cut up

In a 2-qt. saucepan, combine all ingredients except chicken. Bring to a boil, stirring constantly. Reduce heat and simmer, uncovered, for 1 hour, stirring frequently. Remove 1 cup for basting. Store remaining sauce in the refrigerator for another use. Grill chicken, covered, over medium-low coals for 40 minutes or until almost done. Brush with sauce; grill an additional 5 minutes. Turn, brush with sauce and cook until juices run clear. **Yield:** 4 servings.

Baked Chicken on the Grill
Clarice Softing, Hawley, Minnesota

I first made this chicken one hot summer when the family wanted baked chicken...and I wanted to keep the kitchen cool. Now they never seem to request the oven-baked variety!

2/3 cup buttermilk baking mix
1-1/2 teaspoons paprika
1-1/4 teaspoons seasoned salt
1/2 teaspoon pepper
  1 broiler-fryer chicken (3 to 3-1/2 pounds), cut up

Place baking mix, paprika, seasoned salt and pepper in a large resealable plastic bag. Close and shake to mix. Add chicken, a few pieces at a time, and shake to coat. Place

chicken in a greased metal or foil 13-in. x 9-in. x 2-in. baking pan. Place on grill. Cover and grill over low coals, turning once halfway through cooking time, for 60-75 minutes or until juices run clear. **Yield:** 4 servings.

Blackened Cajun Chicken
Marian Platt, Sequim, Washington

My son's a great cook who came up with this rub on his own. It's one of our very favorite ways to prepare chicken because it's nice and zesty.

✓ This tasty dish uses less sugar, salt and fat. Recipe includes *Diabetic Exchanges*.

  1 tablespoon *each* paprika, brown sugar, garlic powder and dry mustard
  1 teaspoon *each* onion powder, ground cumin, dried thyme and pepper
  1 teaspoon crushed bay leaves
  1 teaspoon dried rosemary, crushed
1/2 to 1 teaspoon cayenne pepper
  1 teaspoon salt, optional
  1 broiler-fryer chicken (3 to 3-1/2 pounds), cut up and skin removed

Combine all seasonings. Place chicken in a 13-in. x 9-in. x 2-in. baking dish; rub with half of the seasoning mixture. Cover and refrigerate overnight. Grill, covered, over medium coals, turning once, for 30-45 minutes or until juices run clear. **Yield:** 4 servings. **Editor's Note:** Seasoning mix is enough for two chickens. It may be made ahead and stored in an airtight container until needed. **Diabetic Exchanges:** One serving (prepared without added salt) equals 4 lean meat, 1/2 starch; also, 268 calories, 110 mg sodium, 96 mg cholesterol, 12 gm carbohydrate, 38 gm protein, 8 gm fat.

MILK KEEPS IT MOIST. To keep your barbecued chicken tender and flavorful while grilling, first soak boneless skinless chicken breasts in evaporated milk overnight. Drain, discarding the milk, and prepare chicken as usual.

Perfect-Every-Thyme Marinade
Wayne Snyder, Dalton, Georgia

I prepare this often at shows when demonstrating how to cook on gas grills. People are always pleased with the fantastic flavor. It really is perfect every time!

1/2 cup honey
1/2 cup olive *or* vegetable oil
  1 tablespoon dried thyme
  1 teaspoon garlic salt
  6 boneless skinless chicken breast halves

In a 1-qt. saucepan, combine the first four ingredients; cook over low heat until mixture bubbles and foams, stirring constantly. Remove from heat; cool. Place chicken in a glass baking dish; brush with sauce. Cover and refrigerate overnight. Drain, discarding marinade. Grill chicken, uncovered, over low coals for 10-15 minutes or until juices run clear. **Yield:** 4-6 servings.

SUMMERTIME SPREAD. *Clockwise from top right: Honey-Citrus Chicken Sandwiches, Smoky Grilled Chicken, Supreme Kabobs, Chicken Fajitas and Texas-Style Fryer (all recipes on pages 92 and 93).*

Honey-Citrus Chicken Sandwiches
Claire Batherson, Westchester, Illinois
(PICTURED ON PAGE 91)

During the summer months, our three children keep me plenty busy. So it's a welcome relief when my husband volunteers to cook out. These chicken sandwiches are his specialty!

✓ This tasty dish uses less sugar, salt and fat. Recipe includes *Diabetic Exchanges*.

  6 boneless skinless chicken breast halves
1/4 cup orange juice
1/4 cup lemon juice
1/4 cup honey
  2 tablespoons vegetable oil
  1 tablespoon yellow mustard
1/4 teaspoon poultry seasoning
1/8 to 1/4 teaspoon cayenne pepper
  6 slices Monterey Jack *or* Muenster cheese, optional
  6 kaiser rolls, split
  6 thin tomato slices
  6 red onion slices
Shredded lettuce

Pound chicken breasts until uniform in thickness; set aside. In a large resealable plastic bag or glass 13-in. x 9-in. x 2-in. baking dish, combine orange and lemon juices, honey, oil, mustard, poultry seasoning and cayenne pepper. Add chicken breasts; turn to coat. Cover or close bag and refrigerate for 6-8 hours. Drain, discarding marinade. Grill, uncovered, over medium-low coals, turning occasionally, for 10-12 minutes or until juices run clear. If desired, top each chicken breast with a slice of cheese and grill 1-2 minutes longer or until cheese begins to melt. Serve on rolls with tomato, onion and lettuce. **Yield:** 6 servings. **Diabetic Exchanges:** One serving (prepared without cheese) equals 3 lean meat, 2 starch, 1 vegetable, 1/2 fruit; also, 388 calories, 602 mg sodium, 73 mg cholesterol, 46 gm carbohydrate, 34 gm protein, 8 gm fat.

Smoky Grilled Chicken
Kathy Whipple, Twin Falls, Idaho
(PICTURED ON PAGE 91)

Instant coffee is the "secret" ingredient in this sweet and spicy sauce. Don't be surprised when folks tell you this is the best chicken they've ever had!

1/2 cup packed dark brown sugar
  2 tablespoons dry mustard
  2 tablespoons instant coffee granules
  1 cup hot water
  1 bottle (28 ounces) ketchup
  2 tablespoons liquid smoke
  2 tablespoons Worcestershire sauce
  1 broiler-fryer chicken (3-1/2 to 4 pounds), quartered

In a large bowl, dissolve sugar, mustard and coffee in hot water. Stir in ketchup, liquid smoke and Worcestershire sauce. Reserve 1 cup for basting; refrigerate remaining sauce for another use. Grill chicken, covered,

over medium coals, turning occasionally, for 30 minutes. Brush with sauce. Continue basting and occasionally turning chicken for an additional 15 minutes or until tender and juices run clear. **Yield:** 4 servings.

Chicken Fajitas
Melinda Ewbank, Fairfield, Ohio
(PICTURED ON PAGE 90)

With these colorful fajitas, it's easy to bring a taste of Mexico to your dinner table! The fresh flavor of the grilled meat and peppers appeals to everyone.

✓ This tasty dish uses less sugar, salt and fat. Recipe includes *Diabetic Exchanges*.

  2 tablespoons white wine vinegar
  2 tablespoons fresh lime juice
  1 tablespoon vegetable oil
  1 tablespoon Worcestershire sauce
  1 tablespoon chopped onion
  1 garlic clove, minced
1/2 teaspoon salt, optional
1/2 teaspoon dried oregano
1/4 teaspoon ground cumin
  1 pound boneless skinless chicken breasts
Vegetable oil
  1 medium green pepper, halved and seeded
  1 medium sweet red pepper, halved and seeded
  1 medium sweet onion, sliced
  6 flour tortillas (8 inches)
Salsa
Guacamole, sour cream and shredded cheddar cheese, optional

In a large resealable plastic bag or glass container, combine vinegar, lime juice, oil, Worcestershire sauce, onion, garlic, salt if desired, oregano and cumin. Add chicken. Cover or close bag and refrigerate at least 4 hours. Drain, discarding marinade. Lightly oil vegetables. Grill vegetables and chicken, uncovered, over medium coals for 12-15 minutes or until vegetables begin to soften and chicken juices run clear. Meanwhile, warm tortillas according to package directions. Quickly slice chicken and peppers into strips and separate onion slices into rings. Spoon chicken and vegetables down the center of tortillas; fold in sides. Garnish as desired with salsa, guacamole, sour cream and cheese. **Yield:** 6 servings. **Diabetic Exchanges:** One serving (prepared with low-fat tortillas and without added salt, guacamole, sour cream and cheese) equals 3 lean meat, 1 starch; also, 211 calories, 142 mg sodium, 65 mg cholesterol, 15 gm carbohydrate, 26 gm protein, 5 gm fat.

Texas-Style Fryer
Molly Koepp, Canyon Lake, Texas
(PICTURED ON PAGE 90)

Spring is a special season for us. That's when we invite family and friends over to see the beautiful wildflowers in our backyard and to sample this tender juicy chicken.

  1 tablespoon seasoned salt
  1 teaspoon pepper

1 broiler-fryer chicken (3 to 3-1/2 pounds)
2 garlic cloves, minced
1/2 cup butter *or* margarine
1/2 cup chicken broth
1/4 cup fresh lemon juice

Combine seasoned salt and pepper; rub inside and outside of chicken. Place chicken on rotisserie rod on grill with a drip pan according to manufacturer's directions. In a small saucepan, saute garlic in butter until tender. Stir in broth and lemon juice. Pour into drip pan and place under chicken. Baste with sauce every 15 minutes for 1 to 1-1/2 hours or until juices run clear. Additional broth may be added to basting sauce if necessary. **Yield:** 4 servings.

Lemon and Herb Fryers
Susan Knodel, Idalia, Colorado

With its slight hint of lemon and variety of herbs, this chicken disappears quickly. I'm not sure where this originated, but I've passed it onto countless friends.

3/4 cup vegetable oil
3/4 cup lemon juice
1 tablespoon onion powder
2 teaspoons garlic powder
1-1/2 teaspoons salt
1-1/2 teaspoons celery salt
3/4 teaspoon dried rosemary, crushed
3/4 teaspoon dried thyme
2 broiler-fryer chickens (3 to 3-1/2 pounds *each*), cut up

In two large resealable plastic bags or two glass 13-in. x 9-in. x 2-in. baking dishes, combine the first eight ingredients; mix well. Reserve 1/4 cup; cover. Add chicken to remaining marinade; turn to coat. Cover or close bags and refrigerate at least 12 hours. Drain, discarding marinade. Cover and grill over medium-low coals for 35-45 minutes or until juices run clear. Remove to a serving platter and drizzle with reserved marinade. **Yield:** 8 servings.

Ginger-Glazed Chicken
Wauneva Wagers, Hawarden, Iowa

When I first served this instead of usual fried chicken, my family was hesitant...until they sampled it! Now we alternate between our old standby and our newfound favorite.

3/4 cup barbecue sauce
1/4 cup frozen orange juice concentrate
2 tablespoons brown sugar
1 teaspoon ground ginger
1 broiler-fryer chicken (3 to 3-1/2 pounds), cut up
1/3 cup butter *or* margarine, melted

Combine first four ingredients; set aside. Grill chicken, covered, over medium-low coals, turning and brushing with butter several times, for 30 minutes. Then grill, uncovered, turning and brushing with orange juice mixture several times, for 20-30 minutes or until juices run clear. **Yield:** 4 servings.

Tarragon-Lime Chicken
Brenda Mainwaring, Eden Prairie, Minnesota

The mother of a former boyfriend shared this recipe with me, and I held onto it when the relationship ended! People will rave over this chicken's refreshing, slightly tart taste.

1/2 cup vegetable oil
1/2 cup fresh lime juice
2 tablespoons finely chopped onion
2 teaspoons dried tarragon, crushed
1-1/2 teaspoons salt
1/2 to 1 teaspoon hot pepper sauce
3-1/2 to 4 pounds chicken breast halves (bone in)

In a large resealable plastic bag, combine the first six ingredients; seal and shake. Reserve 1/4 cup for basting; cover and refrigerate. Add chicken to bag. Close bag and refrigerate several hours or overnight. Drain, discarding marinade. Grill chicken, covered, over medium-low coals for 7 minutes. Turn and baste with reserved marinade. Continue cooking and brushing with marinade for 23-38 minutes or until juices run clear. **Yield:** 4-6 servings.

Supreme Kabobs
Karla Gleason, Waterville, Ohio
(PICTURED ON PAGE 91)

I first prepared these splendid skewers at a birthday party... they were an instant success! I especially enjoy serving them for casual weekend meals with friends.

✓ **This tasty dish uses less sugar, salt and fat. Recipe includes** *Diabetic Exchanges.*

3/4 cup vegetable oil
1/3 cup soy sauce
1/4 cup red wine vinegar
1/4 cup fresh lemon juice
2 tablespoons Worcestershire sauce
2 teaspoons dry mustard
1 teaspoon pepper
1 teaspoon dried parsley flakes
2 pounds boneless skinless chicken breasts, cut into 1-inch cubes
12 ounces small fresh mushrooms
1 medium green *or* sweet red pepper, cut into 1-inch pieces
2 small onions, cut into 1-inch pieces
1 can (8 ounces) pineapple chunks, drained

In a large resealable plastic bag or 13-in. x 9-in. x 2-in. glass baking dish, combine first eight ingredients. Add chicken, mushrooms, pepper and onions. Cover or close bag and refrigerate at least 6 hours. Drain, discarding marinade. Thread chicken, vegetables and pineapple alternately on skewers. Grill, covered, over medium-low coals, turning frequently, for 16-20 minutes or until chicken juices run clear. **Yield:** 8 servings. **Diabetic Exchanges:** One serving (prepared with low-sodium soy sauce and unsweetened pineapple) equals 4 lean meat, 1-1/2 vegetable; also, 274 calories, 235 mg sodium, 97 mg cholesterol, 8 gm carbohydrate, 38 gm protein, 9 gm fat.

Dilly Chicken Breasts
Lori Rodman, Ostrander, Ohio

I consider this to be one of my "safe" recipes. No matter how many times I make it, the chicken turns out moist and delicious. It's a guaranteed hit with family and friends.

- 1/2 cup fresh lemon juice
- 1/4 cup butter *or* margarine, melted
- 1 teaspoon salt
- 1 teaspoon dill weed
- 1 teaspoon dried minced onion
- 1/4 teaspoon pepper
- 4 boneless skinless chicken breast halves

In a small bowl, combine all ingredients except chicken. Reserve 1/4 cup for basting; cover. Place chicken in a shallow glass baking dish. Pour remaining sauce over chicken. Marinate for 15 minutes. Drain, discarding marinade. Grill chicken, covered, over medium-low coals, turning and basting with reserved marinade, for 10-15 minutes or until juices run clear. **Yield:** 4 servings.

Jim's Maple Barbecue
Jim Bodle, Canastota, New York

I created this out of my fondness of the maple syrup produced in our state. Your family will like the pleasant sweetness and change of pace from typical sauces.

- 3/4 cup maple syrup
- 1/2 cup vinegar
- 3 tablespoons Worcestershire sauce
- 1 garlic clove
- 4 chicken breast halves (bone in)

In a blender, combine syrup, vinegar, Worcestershire sauce and garlic; process for 30 seconds. Reserve 1/3 cup for basting; cover. Place chicken in a large resealable plastic bag or glass 13-in. x 9-in. x 2-in. baking dish. Pour remaining sauce over chicken. Cover or close bag and refrigerate overnight. Drain, discarding marinade. Grill, covered, over medium-low coals for 40 minutes or until juices run clear, turning and basting with reserved marinade during the last 10 minutes. **Yield:** 4 servings.

Grilled Chicken Kabobs
Sharon Hasty, New London, Missouri

We cook out all four seasons, so, I'm always in search of new marinades. We've been making these marvelous kabobs for years. They're a family favorite.

✓ This tasty dish uses less sugar, salt and fat. Recipe includes *Diabetic Exchanges.*

- 1/2 cup olive *or* vegetable oil
- 1/4 cup lemon juice
- 4 garlic cloves, minced
- 2 teaspoons honey
- 1-1/2 teaspoons dried thyme
- 1 teaspoon crushed red pepper flakes
- 1 teaspoon pepper

- 1 teaspoon salt, optional
- 4 boneless skinless chicken breast halves

In a small bowl, combine oil, lemon juice, garlic, honey, thyme, red pepper flakes, pepper and salt if desired. Reserve half of marinade for basting; cover. Cut chicken into 1-in.-wide strips; weave on skewers. Place in an 11-in. x 7-in. x 2-in. glass baking dish. Pour remaining marinade over chicken. Cover and refrigerate for at least 4 hours. Drain, discarding marinade. Place skewers on grill over medium-low coals. Grill, turning and basting with reserved marinade, for 12 minutes or until juices run clear. **Yield:** 4 servings. **Diabetic Exchanges:** One serving (prepared without added salt) equals 4 lean meat, 1 fat; also, 272 calories, 65 mg sodium, 73 mg cholesterol, 3 gm carbohydrate, 27 gm protein, 17 gm fat.

Garlic Chicken
Karen Kruckenberg, Harvard, Illinois

As a child, I spent countless hours with my mom in the kitchen. Now I do the same with my own daughter. Here's a chicken dish I gradually developed over the years.

✓ This tasty dish uses less sugar, salt and fat. Recipe includes *Diabetic Exchanges.*

- 2 cups buttermilk
- 6 garlic cloves, minced
- 1 teaspoon Worcestershire sauce
- 1/2 teaspoon lemon-pepper seasoning
- 1/2 teaspoon pepper
- 1/4 teaspoon hot pepper sauce
- 1 broiler-fryer chicken (3 to 3-1/2 pounds), cut up
Cayenne pepper

In a large resealable plastic bag or glass 13-in. x 9-in. x 2-in. baking dish, combine the first six ingredients. Add chicken pieces; turn to coat. Cover or close bag and refrigerate at least 8 hours. Drain and shake off excess marinade from chicken; do not rinse. Sprinkle lightly with cayenne pepper. Cover and grill over medium coals, turning once, for 30-45 minutes or until juices run clear. **Yield:** 4 servings. **Diabetic Exchanges:** One serving equals 4 lean meat, 1 vegetable; also, 234 calories, 275 mg sodium, 98 mg cholesterol, 4 gm carbohydrate, 38 gm protein, 6 gm fat.

Basic Chicken Barbecue
Sherry Schmidt, Franklin, Virginia

As far as I'm concerned, there's no better way to spend summer nights than sitting outdoors with the family and enjoying a hot-off-the-grill meal like this.

- 1 cup vinegar
- 1 cup water
- 1/2 cup vegetable oil
- 3 tablespoons sugar
- 2 tablespoons salt
- 1 tablespoon poultry seasoning
- 1 tablespoon pepper
- 1 broiler-fryer chicken (3 to 3-1/2 pounds), cut up

In a small saucepan, combine the first seven ingredients. Bring to a boil; boil for 2 minutes. Allow to cool to lukewarm. Reserve 1/2 cup for basting; cover. Place chicken in a large resealable plastic bag or glass 13-in. x 9-in. x 2-in. baking dish. Pour remaining marinade over chicken. Cover or close bag and refrigerate at least 4 hours. Drain, discarding marinade. Grill, covered, over low coals, turning and brushing with reserved marinade, for 50-60 minutes or until juices run clear. **Yield:** 4 servings.

South-of-the-Border Thighs

Patricia Collins, Imbler, Oregon

We may not live anywhere near the border, but we favor Mexican food! Served with warm tortillas and chili beans, this is a much-requested dish whenever we fire up the grill.

       1 cup olive *or* vegetable oil
 4-1/2 teaspoons chili powder
       1 tablespoon lime juice
       2 teaspoons ground cumin
       1 teaspoon ground coriander
       1 teaspoon salt
    1/2 teaspoon ground cloves
    1/2 teaspoon cayenne pepper
    1/2 teaspoon pepper
       6 garlic cloves, minced
 2-1/2 pounds chicken thighs *or* boneless skinless
         chicken breasts

In a small bowl, combine the first 10 ingredients. Reserve half the marinade for basting; cover. Place chicken in a glass baking dish. Pour remaining marinade over chicken; turn to coat. Cover and refrigerate at least 4 hours. Drain, discarding marinade. Grill chicken, uncovered, over medium-low coals, turning and brushing with reserved marinade, for 20-40 minutes or until juices run clear. **Yield:** 4-6 servings. **Editor's Note:** Watch closely; chicken may burn easily.

Zesty Basil Chicken

Marilyn Hamersley, Gaithersburg, Maryland

The combination of fresh basil and other seasonings gives this chicken a wonderful aroma. It's a real crowd-pleaser at picnics and potlucks...folks always come back for seconds!

✓ This tasty dish uses less sugar, salt and fat. Recipe includes *Diabetic Exchanges.*

 1/3 cup butter *or* margarine, melted
 1/4 cup chopped fresh basil
    1 tablespoon minced onion
    2 garlic cloves, minced
 1/2 teaspoon salt, optional
    4 chicken breast halves (bone in), skin removed
 1/2 teaspoon pepper
 1/2 teaspoon lemon-pepper seasoning
    2 tablespoons grated Parmesan cheese

Combine butter, basil, onion, garlic and salt if desired; mix well. Rub pepper and lemon pepper into chicken. Brush with butter mixture. Grill, covered, over medium-low coals, turning and basting frequently, for 30-45 minutes or until juices run clear. Sprinkle with Parmesan cheese before serving. **Yield:** 4 servings. **Diabetic Exchanges:** One serving (prepared with margarine and

without added salt) equals 4 lean meat, 1 vegetable, 1 fat; also, 303 calories, 562 mg sodium, 75 mg cholesterol, 4 gm carbohydrate, 29 gm protein, 19 gm fat.

Peanut Butter Chicken Skewers

Kari Routledge, Highland, Michigan

A neighbor gave me this recipe, and at first I was skeptical to see peanut butter as an ingredient. But folks can't resist these specially seasoned skewers.

  12 wooden skewers (10 inches)
 1/2 cup chunky peanut butter
 1/2 cup vegetable oil
 1/4 cup white wine vinegar
 1/4 cup soy sauce
 1/4 cup lemon juice
    1 tablespoon brown sugar
    2 teaspoons chili powder *or* crushed red pepper
        flakes
    2 teaspoons ground ginger
    2 garlic cloves
    2 pounds boneless skinless chicken breasts
  12 green onions

Soak skewers in water. Meanwhile, combine the next nine ingredients in a blender or food processor. Blend until smooth, adding a few drops of water if mixture is too thick. Pour into a large resealable plastic bag. Cut chicken into 1-in.-wide strips; add to bag. Close bag and refrigerate for at least 2 hours. Trim 3 in. of green off tops of each onion; cut remaining onion in half. Thread one piece of onion on each skewer. Drain chicken, discarding marinade. Thread two to three strips of chicken on each skewer end with another piece of onion. Grill, uncovered, over medium-low coals, turning every 3-5 minutes, for 15-20 minutes or until juices run clear. **Yield:** 6-8 servings.

Herb-Mustard Chicken

Monell Nuckols, Carpinteria, California

I like to keep dinner interesting at our house. So I'm constantly trying new recipes and asking the family to vote on them. One bite and you'll see why this was a "keeper".

 2/3 cup vegetable oil
 1/2 cup water
 1/3 cup white wine vinegar
 1/4 cup spicy brown mustard
    2 tablespoons finely chopped onion
    1 teaspoon dried thyme *or* Italian seasoning
 1/2 teaspoon salt
 1/2 teaspoon pepper
    2 garlic cloves, minced
    1 broiler-fryer chicken (3 to 3-1/2 pounds), cut up

Combine all ingredients except chicken. Reserve 1/2 cup for basting; cover. Place chicken in a large resealable plastic bag or glass 13-in. x 9-in. x 2-in. baking dish. Pour remaining marinade over chicken. Cover or close bag and refrigerate at least 4 hours. Drain, discarding marinade. Grill, covered, over low coals, turning and basting with reserved marinade every 15 minutes, for 40-50 minutes or until juices run clear. **Yield:** 4 servings.

 # Index

Appetizers
Aunt Shirley's Liver Pate, 6
Buttery Chicken Spread, 7
Cheesy Pecan Roll, 6
Crunchy Chicken Balls, 5
Curried Chicken Cheese Ball, 6
Empanditas, 7
Hot Wings, 6
Sesame Chicken with Honey Sauce, 5
Smoky Chicken Spread, 6
Sweet-and-Sour Chicken Nuggets, 7
Teriyaki Chicken Wings, 5
Tex-Mex Dip, 5

Apples
Brown Rice Apple Salad, 9
Cran-Apple Chicken, 82
Waldorf Salad, 11
Waldorf Sandwiches, 25

Apricots
Almond-Apricot Chicken Salad, 15
Cinnamon-Apricot Chicken Breasts, 67

Asparagus
Asparagus Supreme, 57
Asparagus-Lovers' Stir-Fry, 41
Asparagus-Pecan Quiche, 55
Cheesy Chicken and Asparagus, 40
Chicken and Asparagus, 81
Harvest Chicken, 39
Lemon-Curry Chicken Casserole, 71

Bacon
Bacon and Blue Cheese Chicken, 60
Bacon-Topped Chicken Breasts, 84
California Clubs, 25
Chickenwiches, 27
Fried Chicken Pitas, 27

Barley
Broccoli Barley Saute, 45
Tomato Barley Soup, 23

Beans
Bean, Chicken and Sausage Soup, 25
Chicken Chili, 22
Green Bean Casserole with Biscuits, 79
Hearty Chicken and Beans, 41
Veggie Chicken Chili, 18
Western Drumsticks, 53
White Chili, 18

Berries
Berry Delicious Barbecue, 67
Chicken with Cranberry Compote, 84
Cran-Apple Chicken, 82
Raspberry Basil Chicken, 83

Broccoli
Almond-Apricot Chicken Salad, 15
Black-Eyed Peas Salad, 10
Broccoli Barley Saute, 45
Broccoli Stir-Fry, 53
Broccoli-Cauliflower Toss, 9
Broccoli-Cheese Strata, 76
Broccoli-Chicken Cups, 64
Cheesy Chicken and Rice, 76
Chicken 'n' Rice Salad, 10
Chicken and Broccoli Quiche, 60
Chicken and Pepperoni Pizza, 64
Chicken Broccoli Chowder, 18
Chicken Divan, 77
Chicken with Ginger Sauce, 40
Cordon Bleu Casserole, 73
Deluxe Baked Potatoes, 65
Ginger Chicken Stir-Fry, 49
Lasagna Deluxe, 72
Sausage-Stuffed Chicken, 85
Veggie Chicken Chili, 18

Cabbage/Sauerkraut
German Chicken, 65
Hungarian Cabbage Bake, 68

Casseroles
Broccoli-Cheese Strata, 76
Campfire Casseroles, 88
Cheddar Chicken Mostaccioli, 75
Cheesy Chicken and Rice, 76
Chicken 'n' Noodles for Two, 72
Chicken Almondine, 72
Chicken and Dressing Dish, 76
Chicken and Spinach Supper, 72
Chicken Divan, 77
Chicken Garden Medley, 79
Chicken Livers Royale, 73
Chicken-Mushroom Deluxe, 77
Cordon Bleu Casserole, 73
Corny Bread Bake, 73
Easy Vegetable Casserole, 79
Favorite Hot Chicken Salad, 77
Green Bean Casserole with Biscuits, 79
Lasagna Deluxe, 72
Lemon-Curry Chicken Casserole, 71
Overnight Noodle Toss, 77
Party Casserole, 75
Savory-Crust Chicken Pie, 71
Speedy Scalloped Potatoes, 76
Summer Squash Enchiladas, 71
Swiss Chicken Bake, 75

Cauliflower
Broccoli-Cauliflower Toss, 9
Ginger Chicken Stir-Fry, 49

Cheese
Bacon and Blue Cheese Chicken, 60
Broccoli-Cheese Strata, 76
Cheddar Chicken Mostaccioli, 75
Cheesy Chicken and Asparagus, 40
Cheesy Chicken and Rice, 76
Cheesy Chicken Crepes, 83
Cheesy Chicken Roll-Ups, 56
Cheesy Pasta Salad, 14
Cheesy Pecan Roll, 6
Cheesy Tortilla Soup, 19
Chicken Mozzarella, 64
Chicken Parmesan, 37
Cordon Bleu Casserole, 73
Curried Chicken Cheese Ball, 6
Swiss Chicken Bake, 75
Three-Cheese Nachos, 7
Tortilla Chicken with Cheese Sauce, 32

Chicken Livers
Aunt Shirley's Liver Pate, 6
Chicken Livers Royale, 73

Chili
Chicken Chili, 22
Veggie Chicken Chili, 18
White Chili, 18

Chowder
Chicken Broccoli Chowder, 18
Southwestern Corn Chowder, 22
Zesty Corn Chowder, 23

Corn
Chicken and Corn Medley, 51
Corny Bread Bake, 73
Southwestern Corn Chowder, 22
Western Drumsticks, 53
Zesty Corn Chowder, 23

Corn Bread
Chicken Tamale Pie, 79
Corny Bread Bake, 73
Zesty Corn Bread with Creamed
   Chicken, 69

Diabetic Exchange Recipes
*(Lower in salt, sugar and fat,
and evaluated for diabetics)*

Blackened Cajun Chicken, 89
Broccoli Barley Saute, 45
Broccoli Stir-Fry, 53
Chicken 'n' Peppers, 40
Chicken and Asparagus, 81
Chicken and Dressing Dish, 76
Chicken and Spinach Supper, 72
Chicken and Tomato Scampi, 44
Chicken Chili, 22
Chicken Divan, 77
Chicken Fajitas, 92
Chicken-Mushroom Loaf, 56
Chunky Chicken Soup, 23
Crunchy Chicken Balls, 5
Curried Chicken Cheese Ball, 6
Favorite Skillet Dinner, 41
15-Minute Marinated Chicken, 88

Garlic Chicken, 94
Garlic-Lime Chicken, 87
Ginger Chicken Stir-Fry, 49
Granny's Spicy Soup, 27
Grilled Chicken Kabobs, 94
Grilled Chicken Salad, 15
Grilled Curry Chicken, 88
Harvest Chicken Rice Soup, 17
Harvest Chicken, 39
Herbed Chicken Soup, 25
Herbed Chicken, 69
Honey-Citrus Chicken Sandwiches, 92
Mom's Tomato Vegetable Soup, 19
Oatmeal Baked Chicken, 35
Orange Chicken, 55
Picante Chicken, 44
Spicy Chicken Saute, 52
Stir-Fry Spinach Salad, 13
Supreme Kabobs, 93
Swedish Potato Dumpling Soup, 26
Tex-Mex Chicken Soup, 29
30-Minute Chicken, 61
Tomato Barley Soup, 23
Vegetable Chicken, 59
Veggie Chicken Chili, 18
White Chili, 18
Zesty Basil Chicken, 95
Zesty Chicken and Rice, 60

Dumplings

Chicken 'n' Dumplings with Sour
    Cream Gravy, 43
Chicken Stew with Dumplings, 45
Grandma's Chicken 'n' Dumpling
    Soup, 29
Matzo Ball Soup, 26
Swedish Potato Dumpling Soup, 26

Fried Chicken

Baked Crumbled Chicken, 32
Chicken Parmesan, 37
Coconut Chicken with Pineapple
    Vinaigrette, 35
Creamy Pan-Fried Chicken, 31
Creole Fried Chicken, 37
Extra-Crispy Italian Chicken, 37
Famous Fried Chicken, 35
Ginger Batter Chicken, 33
Golden Chicken, 33
Herbed Chicken with Mustard Sauce, 33
Horse-Show Chicken, 37
Marinated Baked Chicken Breasts, 33
Mustard Drumsticks for Two, 31
Oatmeal Baked Chicken, 35
Onion-Baked Chicken, 36
Oven-Baked Sesame Chicken, 35
Pecan Oven-Fried Fryer, 36
Picnic Potato Chip Chicken, 31
Ranch-Style Thighs, 36
Saucy Skillet Chicken, 37
Savory Seasoned Chicken, 32

Sesame Fried Chicken, 36
Southern-Fried Fryer, 31
Sweet 'n' Nutty Fried Chicken, 32
Tasty Texas Tenders, 36
Tortilla Chicken with Cheese Sauce, 32

Fruits

(also see specific kinds)

Fruit-Glazed Roast Chicken, 81
Fruity Rice Salad, 13
Melon Salad with Ginger Dressing, 13
Summertime Salad with Honey
    Dressing, 11
Tropical Chicken Bake, 61
Tropical Fruit Medley, 10

Grilled Chicken

Baked Chicken on the Grill, 89
Basic Chicken Barbecue, 94
Blackened Cajun Chicken, 89
Campfire Casseroles, 88
Caribbean Delight, 88
Chicken Fajitas, 92
Dad's Best Barbecue, 87
Dilly Chicken Breasts, 94
15-Minute Marinated Chicken, 88
Garlic Chicken, 94
Garlic-Lime Chicken, 87
Ginger-Glazed Chicken, 93
Grilled Chicken Kabobs, 94
Grilled Chicken Salad, 15
Grilled Curry Chicken, 88
Herb-Mustard Chicken, 95
Honey-Citrus Chicken Sandwiches, 92
Honey-Mustard Chicken, 87
Jim's Maple Barbecue, 94
Lemon and Herb Fryers, 93
Mexican Grilled Chicken, 88
Mustard-Lover's Grilled Chicken, 87
Peanut Butter Chicken Skewers, 95
Perfect-Every-Thyme Marinade, 89
Saucy Barbecued Chicken, 89
Smoky Grilled Chicken, 92
South-of-the-Border Thighs, 95
Supreme Kabobs, 93
Tarragon-Lime Chicken, 93
Teriyaki Chicken Sandwiches, 22
Texas-Style Fryer, 92
Zesty Basil Chicken, 95

Ham

Chicken and Ham Roll-Ups, 84
Cordon Bleu Casserole, 73
Garlic Chicken Fried Rice, 51
Harvest Stuffed Chicken, 67

Honey

Honey Lime Chicken, 48
Honey-Citrus Chicken Sandwiches, 92
Honey-Mustard Chicken, 87
Sesame Chicken with Honey Sauce, 5
Summertime Salad with Honey
    Dressing, 11

Lemon

Honey-Citrus Chicken Sandwiches, 92

Lemon Almond Chicken, 82
Lemon and Herb Fryers, 93
Lemon-Curry Chicken Casserole, 71
Lemony Chicken Salad, 15
Sunshine Chicken, 59

Lime

Caribbean Delight, 88
Garlic-Lime Chicken, 87
Honey Lime Chicken, 48
Key Lime Thighs, 64
Tarragon-Lime Chicken, 93

Meat Pies/Pizzas

Asparagus-Pecan Quiche, 55
Chicken and Broccoli Quiche, 60
Chicken and Pepperoni Pizza, 64
Chicken Pizzas, 68
Chicken Potpie, 56
Chicken Tamale Pie, 79
Texas Pie, 73
Veggie-Stuffed Pizza Bread, 57

Microwave Recipes

Cheesy Chicken Roll-Ups, 56
Chicken and Ham Roll-Ups, 84
Herbed Chicken, 69

Mushrooms

Baked Chicken Sandwiches with
    Mushroom Sauce, 26
Baked Chicken with Mushroom
    Gravy, 59
Chicken-Mushroom Deluxe, 77
Chicken-Mushroom Loaf, 56

Mustard

Herb-Mustard Chicken, 95
Herbed Chicken with Mustard
    Sauce, 33
Honey-Mustard Chicken, 87
15-Minute Marinated Chicken, 88
Mustard Drumsticks for Two, 31
Mustard-Lover's Grilled Chicken, 87

Nuts

Almond-Apricot Chicken Salad, 15
Cheesy Pecan Roll, 6
Chicken Almondine, 72
Lemon Almond Chicken, 82
Minnesota Wild Rice Salad, 11
Pecan Oven-Fried Fryer, 36

Nuts (continued)
Pecan Poultry Stuffing, 83
Smoky Chicken Spread, 6
Waldorf Salad, 11
Waldorf Sandwiches, 25

Orange

Chicken Salad Supreme, 10
Garden Party Salad, 11
Ginger-Glazed Chicken, 93
Honey-Citrus Chicken Sandwiches, 92
Orange Chicken, 55
Orange Pasta Salad, 14
Orange-Coated Chicken, 61
South Seas Skillet, 51
Tropical Chicken Bake, 61

Oven Dishes

*(also see Casseroles, Meat Pies/Pizzas
and Microwave Recipes)*
Asparagus Supreme, 57
Bacon and Blue Cheese Chicken, 60
Bacon-Topped Chicken Breasts, 84
Baked Chicken with Mushroom
    Gravy, 59
Berry Delicious Barbecue, 67
Broccoli-Chicken Cups, 64
Cheesy Chicken Crepes, 83
Cheesy Chicken Roll-Ups, 56
Chicken and Asparagus, 81
Chicken and Ham Roll-Ups, 84
Chicken Barbecued in Foil, 65
Chicken Florentine, 82
Chicken Lasagna Rolls, 85
Chicken Mozzarella, 64
Chicken Rice Balls, 60
Chicken-Mushroom Loaf, 56
Cinnamon-Apricot Chicken Breasts, 67
Cran-Apple Chicken, 82
Creamy Chicken and Vegetables, 69
Crowd-Pleasing Rice Bake, 68
Curried Chicken and Rice, 85
Deluxe Baked Potatoes, 65
Dijon Chicken, 81
Fruit-Glazed Roast Chicken, 81
German Chicken, 65
Harvest Stuffed Chicken, 67
Harvest Vegetable Bake, 57
Herbed Chicken, 69
Hungarian Cabbage Bake, 68
Italian-Style Supper, 60
Key Lime Thighs, 64
Lemon Almond Chicken, 82
Mexican-Style Chicken Kiev, 84
Orange Chicken, 55
Orange-Coated Chicken, 61
Peach-Glazed Chicken, 61
Peachy Chicken, 67
Pecan Poultry Stuffing, 83
Raspberry Basil Chicken, 83
Roasted Chicken with Brown Gravy, 64
Roasted Chicken with Sausage
    Stuffing, 56

Saucy Muffin Cups, 68
Sausage-Stuffed Chicken, 85
Simply Great Chicken, 55
Spinach-Stuffed Chicken Breasts, 82
Sunshine Chicken, 59
Sweet Smoky Chicken Legs, 55
Sweet-and-Sour Baked Chicken, 59
30-Minute Chicken, 61
Tropical Chicken Bake, 61
Vegetable Chicken, 59
Zesty Chicken and Rice, 60
Zesty Corn Bread with Creamed
    Chicken, 69

Pasta

Almond-Apricot Chicken Salad, 15
Cheddar Chicken Mostaccioli, 75
Cheesy Pasta Salad, 14
Chicken 'n' Noodles for Two, 72
Chicken and Peas with Pasta, 48
Chicken Garden Medley, 79
Chicken Lasagna Rolls, 85
Chicken Potpie, 56
Chicken Soup with Stuffed Noodles, 17
Chicken-Mushroom Deluxe, 77
Chunky Chicken Soup, 23
Eggplant Provencale, 43
Granny's Spicy Soup, 27
Herbed Chicken Soup, 25
Lasagna Deluxe, 72
Matzo Ball Soup, 26
Mediterranean Chicken, 45
Orange Pasta Salad, 14
Overnight Noodle Toss, 77
Swedish Potato Dumpling Soup, 26
Swiss Chicken Bake, 75

Peaches

Peach-Glazed Chicken, 61
Peachy Chicken, 67

Peas

Black-Eyed Peas Salad, 10
Chicken and Peas with Pasta, 48

Peppers

Chicken 'n' Peppers, 40
Chicken Fajitas, 92
Pepper Chicken and Rice, 39
Supreme Kabobs, 93
Sweet-and-Sour Chicken, 52

Pineapple

Coconut Chicken with Pineapple
    Vinaigrette, 35
Grilled Chicken Salad, 15
Honey Lime Chicken, 48
Stir-Fry Spinach Salad, 13
Supreme Kabobs, 93
Sweet-and-Sour Chicken, 52
Waldorf Sandwiches, 25

Potatoes

Campfire Casseroles, 88
Chicken Sausage Saute, 43
Chicken Stew with Dumplings, 45
Creamy Chicken Stew, 40

Deluxe Baked Potatoes, 65
Dilly Chicken and Potatoes, 44
Favorite Skillet Dinner, 41
Grandma's Chicken 'n' Dumpling
    Soup, 29
Harvest Chicken Rice Soup, 17
Harvest Chicken, 39
Harvest Vegetable Bake, 57
Herbed Chicken, 69
Italian-Style Supper, 60
Mom's Tomato Vegetable Soup, 19
Speedy Scalloped Potatoes, 76

Rice

Asparagus Supreme, 57
Asparagus-Lovers' Stir-Fry, 41
Black-Eyed Peas Salad, 10
Brown Rice Apple Salad, 9
Cheesy Chicken and Rice, 76
Chicken 'n' Rice Salad, 10
Chicken Almondine, 72
Chicken and Ham Roll-Ups, 84
Chicken Pilaf Saute, 49
Chicken Rice Balls, 60
Chicken Salad Supreme, 10
Chicken-Mushroom Loaf, 56
Cinnamon-Apricot Chicken Breasts, 67
Crowd-Pleasing Rice Bake, 68
Curried Chicken and Rice, 85
Easy Fried Rice, 53
Favorite Hot Chicken Salad, 77
Fiesta Salad, 14
Fruity Rice Salad, 13
Garlic Chicken Fried Rice, 51
Harvest Chicken Rice Soup, 17
Hearty Chicken and Beans, 41
Mediterranean Chicken, 45
Minnesota Wild Rice Salad, 11
Pepper Chicken and Rice, 39
Quick Skillet Chicken, 48
South Seas Skillet, 51
Sweet-and-Sour Chicken, 52
Tomato Barley Soup, 23
Wild Rice Soup, 29
Zesty Chicken and Rice, 60

Salads

Almond-Apricot Chicken Salad, 15
Black-Eyed Peas Salad, 10
Broccoli-Cauliflower Toss, 9
Brown Rice Apple Salad, 9
Cheesy Pasta Salad, 14
Chicken 'n' Rice Salad, 10
Chicken Caesar Salad, 9
Chicken Salad Supreme, 10
Creamy Chicken Crunch, 13
Fiesta Salad, 14
Fruity Rice Salad, 13
Garden Party Salad, 11
Greek Chicken Salad, 10
Grilled Chicken Salad, 15
Lemony Chicken Salad, 15

Melon Salad with Ginger Dressing, 13
Minnesota Wild Rice Salad, 11
Orange Pasta Salad, 14
Overnight Chicken Fruit Salad, 14
Southern-Style Chicken Salad, 15
Spicy Barbecue Chicken Salad, 9
Stir-Fry Spinach Salad, 13
Summertime Salad with Honey
    Dressing, 11
Susan's Stuffed Tomatoes, 11
Tarragon Chicken Salad, 14
Tropical Fruit Medley, 10
Waldorf Salad, 11

Sandwiches

Baked Chicken Sandwiches with
    Mushroom Sauce, 26
Barbecued Chicken Sandwiches, 17
California Clubs, 25
Chicken Burgers, 19
Chicken Fajitas, 92
Chickenwiches, 27
Curried Chicken Turnovers, 22
Fried Chicken Pitas, 27
Honey-Citrus Chicken Sandwiches, 92
Hot Chicken Heroes, 23
Make-Ahead Saucy Sandwiches, 27
Stir-Fried Chicken Fajitas, 52
Teriyaki Chicken Sandwiches, 22
Veggie-Stuffed Pizza Bread, 57
Waldorf Sandwiches, 25

Sausage

Bean, Chicken and Sausage Soup, 25
Chicken Sausage Saute, 43
Roasted Chicken with Sausage
    Stuffing, 56
Sausage-Stuffed Chicken, 85
Smoked Sausage Soup, 18
Crowd-Pleasing Rice Bake, 68

Skillets/Stir-Frys

Asparagus-Lovers' Stir-Fry, 41
Broccoli Barley Saute, 45
Broccoli Stir-Fry, 53
Cheesy Chicken and Asparagus, 40
Chicken 'n' Dumplings with Sour
    Cream Gravy, 43
Chicken 'n' Peppers, 40
Chicken a la King, 44
Chicken and Corn Medley, 51
Chicken and Peas with Pasta, 48
Chicken and Tomato Scampi, 44

Chicken Italiano, 49
Chicken Piccata, 45
Chicken Pilaf Saute, 49
Chicken Sausage Saute, 43
Chicken with Cranberry Compote, 84
Chicken with Cucumber Sauce, 49
Chicken with Ginger Sauce, 40
Cola Chicken, 43
Dilly Chicken and Potatoes, 44
Easy Chicken Creole, 48
Easy Fried Rice, 53
Eggplant Provencale, 43
Favorite Skillet Dinner, 41
Garlic Chicken Fried Rice, 51
Garlic-Brown Sugar Chicken, 51
Ginger Chicken Stir-Fry, 49
Harvest Chicken, 39
Hearty Chicken and Beans, 41
Honey Lime Chicken, 48
Mediterranean Chicken, 45
Pepper Chicken and Rice, 39
Picante Chicken, 44
Quick Skillet Chicken, 48
Sesame Chicken, 39
Skillet Chicken and Vegetables, 52
Smothered Ginger Chicken, 53
South Seas Skillet, 51
Spicy Chicken Saute, 52
Stir-Fried Chicken Fajitas, 52
Stir-Fry Spinach Salad, 13
Sweet-and-Sour Chicken, 52
Western Drumsticks, 53

Soups

(also see Chili and Chowder)

Bean, Chicken and Sausage Soup, 25
Cheesy Tortilla Soup, 19
Chicken Soup with Stuffed Noodles, 17
Chunky Chicken Soup, 23
Grandma's Chicken 'n' Dumpling
    Soup, 29
Granny's Spicy Soup, 27
Harvest Chicken Rice Soup, 17
Herbed Chicken Soup, 25
Matzo Ball Soup, 26
Mom's Tomato Vegetable Soup, 19
Smoked Sausage Soup, 18
Swedish Potato Dumpling Soup, 26
Tex-Mex Chicken Soup, 29
Tomato Barley Soup, 23
Wild Rice Soup, 29

Spinach

Bacon-Topped Chicken Breasts, 84
Chicken and Spinach Supper, 72
Chicken Florentine, 82
Chicken Lasgana Rolls, 85
Spinach-Stuffed Chicken Breasts, 82
Stir-Fry Spinach Salad, 13
Swiss Chicken Bake, 75

Squash

Chicken Garden Medley, 79
Party Casserole, 75
Skillet Chicken and Vegetables, 52
Smoked Sausage Soup, 18
Summer Squash Enchiladas, 71
Tex-Mex Chicken Soup, 29
30-Minute Chicken, 61

Stews

Chicken Stew with Dumplings, 45
Creamy Chicken Stew, 40

Stuffing/Dressing

Chicken Almondine, 72
Chicken and Dressing Dish, 76
Pecan Poultry Stuffing, 83
Roasted Chicken with Sausage
    Stuffing, 56

Sweet Potatoes

Harvest Chicken Rice Soup, 17
Tropical Chicken Bake, 61

Tomatoes

Chicken and Tomato Scampi, 44
Mom's Tomato Vegetable Soup, 19
Susan's Stuffed Tomatoes, 11
Tomato Barley Soup, 23

Vegetables

(also see specific kinds)

Campfire Casseroles, 88
Chicken Potpie, 56
Chicken with Cucumber Sauce, 49
Creamy Chicken and Vegetables, 69
Easy Fried Rice, 53
Easy Vegetable Casserole, 79
Eggplant Provencale, 43
Favorite Skillet Dinner, 41
Harvest Vegetable Bake, 57
Overnight Noodle Toss, 77
Skillet Chicken and Vegetables, 52
Vegetable Chicken, 59
Veggie Chicken Chili, 18
Veggie-Stuffed Pizza Bread, 57
Chicken Garden Medley, 79